From the Furnace, with Love

The Multigenerational Tapestry of Shirley Cavanaugh

The 28-Year-Old Sex Worker Who Toppled the 1950s Pittsburgh
Vice Squad and Why Her Story Still Matters Today

Author: Jason Kirin
Editor: Dana Kaufman

ISBN: 979-8-9878496-2-0 (Paperback)
ISBN: 979-8-9878496-3-7 (Digital)
ISBN: 979-8-9878496-4-4 (Full Color Hardback Edition)

Front cover design and layout by Kelly Day.

Self-published through IngramSpark

First printed edition: December 17th, 2023
The International Day to End Violence Against Sex Workers.

Part One: Just a Coincidence.................................7

   136 6th St...10

   Lt. Allen Carnahan and The ABA......................12

   Shirley Virginia Cavanaugh..........................15

   Marriage to Walter Lauterbach.......................20

   A Night Off at The Hollywood Show Bar...............24

   The Burglary..28

   Eugene Coon
   (... he forgot to duck ...)......................34

   From the Furnace, with Love.........................39

   The Rockiest of Love Affairs........................43

   The Carnahan Affair.................................48

   Louis Rosenberg.....................................49

   The Teitelbaum Probe................................138

   Life After The Carnahan Affair......................150

   The Final Days of Shirley Cavanaugh.................154

Part Two: An Unjust Coincidence...................159

   James Russell Garretson.............................161

   Ruth Alma Cavanaugh.................................165

   Ruth Elsa Horensky..................................169

   Backstage Disco at the Holiday House................171

   Ruth Elsa Kirin.....................................175

   Judy Louise Lauterbach..............................180

   Forrest Dorsey Garretson III........................187

   The Unfracturing Family.............................194

   1996 - 1999 "The Shirley Cavanaugh Story"
   (The Book That Was Never Written)...................199

   Chasing Family......................................206

   2001 - 2003 Back to New Orleans.....................214

   May 2003 - Back to Pittsburgh.......................221

   The End of an Era...................................222

Part Three: A Just Coincidence....................225

   2022 - 2023 "From The Furnace With Love"
   (The Book That Was Written).........................227

The Past Isn't What It Used to Be.............................252
From Bullet to Box Step..261
Where to Donate in Shirley Cavanaugh's Name.........264
Acknowledgments...267
Genogram..283
Photo Gallery...284
Contact and Social Media Info..................................299

Dedication

Forrest Dorsey Garretson III

May this be the second book in circulation to bear your memory.

The story you are about to read is entirely true —

and it starts with a lie.

Part One: Just a Coincidence

The etymology of coincidence can be traced back to the 1600s, from the Medieval Latin *coincidere*. Meaning: to fall upon a moment, together.

In the 1970s, the paths of two individuals named Bruce and Ruth intersected, for the first time, at a single, shared, fallen moment.

Bruce, a wrestler, football player, and engineer by profession and education, decided one day to do something that scared him: take dance lessons. Accordingly, he signed up for classes at Arthur Murray's Dance Studio, downtown Pittsburgh.

Concomitantly, Ruth, an artist passionate about beauty and movement, attended the Pittsburgh Beauty Academy in the mid-70s for a cosmetology license. After graduation, as she maintained the dream of owning her own beauty salon, she took up a position teaching ballroom, salsa, and tango at that same dance studio.

Coincidentally, they became teacher and student.

But how innumerable the paths must have been to have led to that moment.

That single, shared moment where two tales coalesced into one to tell parallel stories for the next few decades. How multitudinous the coincidences required to have led either of them to that location, at that moment in time, together.

Considering the phrase "it's just a coincidence," it's a wonder why these moments are brushed off as *just* anything. A coincidence inspires those willing to witness it to stretch the limits of subjective meaning, allowing them to bridge the distance between knowing and not knowing. A coincidence is neutral — an occurrence that remains meaningless until one takes notice of its moments and ascribes significance to them.

One moment of significance occurred in 1955: at two years old, Ruth was found alone, malnourished, and dehydrated in her crib. Her mother, Shirley Cavanaugh, was nowhere to be found. Unable to care for herself, Ruth was adopted by her great-aunt and great-uncle, Elsa and Art Horensky.

Two years later, on Sunday, February 24th, 1957, at approximately 6 a.m., Acting Lieutenant Allen Carnahan, head of the Pittsburgh Vice and Narcotic Squad, stopped into The Athletic Boosters Association at 136 6th St. to get a cup of coffee and instead — shot himself in the groin.

And by coincidence only, all of these stories, all of these moments ... they intersect.

136 6th St.

In the early 1900s, as downtown Pittsburgh grew as both a business and entertainment district, 136 6th St. was found securely in the center. Located equidistant to each glittering theater and hotbed hotel, a strangely *distinct* and almost intimate energy began to rarify within the brick structure.

North View May 16, 1915

136 6th Street

[Pittsburgh City Photographer Collection 1901 - 2000]

As early as 1911, ads in multiple newspapers were found not only for a large toy store, men's clothing store, and shoe store, but also a wholesale millinery company which boasted their inventory contained "hats of every description, shape, and color." Most importantly, all of their hats were transcendent and *only* for women.

A list of restaurants, equally unique in names and claims, were graced with 136 6th St. upon their masthead. Restaurants such as Black's Devil Cave, Black's Pala Royale, The Bamboo Inn, Famous Coffee Dan's, The Spaghetti Village, and LaGalondrina.

Not to mention the slew of slick clubs such as the New Ritz Billiard Parlor, Club 30, and The Athletic Boosters Association.

Or The ABA for short, where this story begins.

Precisely, the morning of February 24th, 1957 …

Lt. Allen Carnahan and The ABA

Marihuana Source Traced

BACKYARD PATCH—Lieutenant Allen Carnahan, of the police narcotic squad, is shown above pointing to a marihuana plant growing in the backyard of ▮▮▮▮▮▮▮▮. It was discovered at daylight yesterday after police reported finding enough of the weed in Myers' auto to make 250 "reefers." He faces a preliminary hearing today.

Pittsburgh Post-Gazette, July 4, 1955

Acting Lieutenant Allen Carnahan, head of the Pittsburgh Vice and Narcotic Squad from 1952 to 1957, was known not only as an immaculate dresser, but also an immaculate policeman, one who earned the highest marks from the Federal Bureau of Narcotics' school in Washington and was described by the Pittsburgh Assistant District Attorney, Robert McGee, as "the best policeman I ever knew."

"In our contacts," McGee continued, "Lieutenant Carnahan impressed me as being not only intelligent and industrious, but a gentleman. You don't get that combination very often in a policeman. Since he's been in charge of the narcotics squad they've really learned how to investigate and prepare a case. Every case they brought in was done up properly." [1]

Married in 1934, Allen's wife, Agnes, would describe him as a "good man who hasn't changed in 22 years." [2] However, on February 24th, 1957, Allen would have to accept that change — was inescapable.

At 6 a.m., while working the beat in downtown Pittsburgh, Allen entered The Athletic Boosters Association at 136 6th St. to get a cup of coffee. As he sat on the barstool, Allen moved his .38 caliber service revolver from his left coat pocket to his right hip holster.

During this transition, Carnahan's revolver discharged unexpectedly and accidentally.

12

A bullet was fired and tore through his right thigh and groin before lodging itself in his left thigh.

Carnahan collapsed in pain, bleeding onto the barroom floor.

The following day the *Pittsburgh Post-Gazette*, the *Record-Argus*, the *Daily American*, and the *Pittsburgh Sun-Telegraph* all reported identical details: Carnahan was "working on something." The shot was a self-inflicted accident. And Carnahan recovered in Allegheny General Hospital where all doctors reported his condition as "satisfactory." [3][4][5][6]

City Dope Squad Chief

Cop Shot With Own Gun

Carnahan Wounded in Downtown Club During 6 A. M. Coffee Break

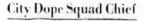

Acting Lieutenant Allen Carnahan, head of the city's narcotic squad, was wounded seriously with his own service revolver yesterday morning in a Downtown club.

The bullet from the .38 caliber weapon went through the u p p e r right thigh, through the groin and lodged in the left thigh.

The shooting, the 46-year-old officer said, occurred when the weapon discharged accidentally as he was switching it from his left coat pocket to his right hip pocket.

Police said the shooting occurred in the Athletic Boosters Association at 134 Sixth Street at 6 a. m. where Carnahan told police, he had stopped for a cup of coffee.

The wounded officer was taken to Allegheny General Hospital where the bullet was removed. Despite the severity of the wound, doctors said the bullet missed both thigh bones and described Carnahan's general condition as "good."

Lieutenant Francis Walsh, the first officer to reach the scene, quoted Carnahan as saying: "I was working on something." The indications

were, police said, that the investigation was prior to entering the club.

Walsh said Carnahan was lying on the floor, in intense pain, and there were only six men—officials or waiters—there when he arrived. They were engaged in cleaning up the club which Carnahan said was closed when he was admitted.

Carnahan gave substantially the same report of the shooting, to Assistant Superintendent Lawrence J. Maloney later at the hospital. He told Maloney he was sitting on a bar stool when his gun went off and the force knocked him to the floor.

Pete Kyrimes, secretary of the club, also told police Carnahan came in for a cup of coffee while bartenders and waiters were cleaning up.

"I heard a shot and he went off the stool," Kyrimes said.

LT. CARNAHAN
Shot in Downtown club.

Neither Kyrimes nor others there admitted seeing the actual shooting, Maloney said.

The club—commonly known as the ABA—formerly was (Continued on Page 4, Col. 6)

Pittsburgh Post-Gazette, Feb. 25, 1957

13

[1] "Assistant DA Points to Record: Carnahan Rated No. 1 Officer." *The Pittsburgh Press*, 27 Feb. 1957, P. 1, Col. 6-8. https://www.newspapers.com/image/148007997.

[2] "I know Al, He's Good, Wife Says." *Pittsburgh Sun-Telegraph*, 3 Mar. 1957, P. 1, Col. 4. https://www.newspapers.com/image/524003125.

[3] "Pennsylvania News Briefs." *Record-Argus*, 25 Feb. 1957, P. 12, Col. 5. https://www.newspapers.com/image/10926009.

[4] "Cop Shot With Own Gun." *Pittsburgh Post-Gazette*, 25 Feb. 1957, P. 1, Col. 2. https://www.newspapers.com/image/90017904.

[5] "Lt. Carnahan is Accidentally Shot by Own Revolver." *Daily American*, 25 Feb. 1957, P. 7, Col. 7. https://www.newspapers.com/image/511094283.

[6] "Lt. Carnahan Wounds Self: Own Gun Goes Off." *Pittsburgh Sun-Telegraph*, 25 Feb. 1957, P. 13, Col. 9, https://www.newspapers.com/image/524002899.

Shirley Virginia Cavanaugh

The Great Crash of 1929 that signified the start of the Great Depression was a slow collapse that began September 4th, 1929, and ended roughly two months later, on November 13th, 1929. Instigating a decade-long, worldwide, economic depression.

Into that world, one year earlier, on Tuesday, November 12th, 1928, Shirley Virginia Cavanaugh was born.

From census data, ancestry research, family narratives, and interviews given by Shirley to various news outlets in the 1950s, it was possible to build, and verify, a fairly accurate timeline of her life using her own words.

Born to parents Frank and Alma Cavanaugh (née Horensky), Shirley, the oldest of three children, spent her youth impoverished in the polluted industrial suburbs of Braddock, PA.

Alma & Frank Cavanaugh

[Shirley's personal collection]

Audrey, Francis, Shirley & Alma Cavanaugh

[Shirley's personal collection]

In 1940, when Shirley was 12, Frank disappeared, leaving Alma, Shirley's mother, to take care of her three children alone.[1] Consequently, Alma found she was incapable of doing just that and, on August 10th, 1942, placed Shirley, age 13, Francis, age 12, and Audrey, age 9, in the Zelienople Orphan's Home. [1]

Shirley later explained, "... my mother's a good woman, but she couldn't take care of us." [2]

Within a few years Alma, a newly single woman, met a man named Chuck Hall and remarried. Perhaps given a renewed sense of security, Alma went back to the Zelienople Orphan's Home and retrieved Shirley and Audrey. But not Francis. She moved her and her daughters into a new home with a new life, and with new in-laws.

As a result, Shirley found herself, Audrey and her mother, sharing a four-room apartment with seven family members. Three of them, Chuck and his parents, were absolute strangers to her. [2]

In the background of her life, on May 27th, 1944, Frank Cavanaugh, Shirley's estranged father, died. She was 16. [3]

Unsurprisingly, Alma found herself struggling to care for her children as she continued to live under such strained domestic conditions and married to a man who was, reportedly, often abusive to not only her, but also to Shirley and Audrey. [4] Alma existed in a society, and family, entirely devoid of supportive resources. So she made a decision.

"That's when she had me put in Gumbert,[2]" Shirley explains:

---

[1] Interviews with multiple family members suggest Frank made this separation, and life, in general, quite toxic for the entire family.

[2] A county school for delinquent girls in operation from 1925-1961, in McCandless Township, Pennsylvania. [4]

"I don't remember what year it was. It was around November 12th, my birthday. I ran away from home to get a job and my mother called Gumbert School. The probation officer came down for me. I had just gotten a job in the restaurant of a bus depot in Greenville, S.C. when the police walked in for me.[3] She went to the Juvenile Court. I don't think it was because I was truant from school. She just couldn't take care of all of us.[4]" [2]

Shirley spent the remainder of her adolescence and later teenage years moving between Gumbert, The Home of the Good Shepherd,[5] and, ultimately, the State Training School at Morganza .[6] [2]

On July 20th, 1948, Francis, Shirley's brother, enlisted and departed for the Army. [7]

However, in 1950, an interlude to instability occurred. A coincidence. Audrey, Shirley's sister, set her up on a blind date with Walter Lauterbach. A taxi-driver, musician, and Hospital Corpsman Second Class for the U.S. Navy. [8]

Shirley found momentary respite to her chaos as she fell into the arms of love.

---

[3] Alma and Chuck may have lived briefly in SC. Shirley may have also, simply, been a run away. Family narratives suggest both as possibilities.

[4] At this point, "all of us" would have included Chuck and Alma's two boys, Chuckie and Georgie, as well.

[5] An orphanage for girls and young women that opened in 1872. While its location and mission have both broadened. Home of the Good Shepherd is still in operation today. [5]

[6] Also known as the Western Center, Morganza was a state-run mental hospital and reform school near Canonsburg, Pennsylvania in operation from 1850 to 1998. [6]

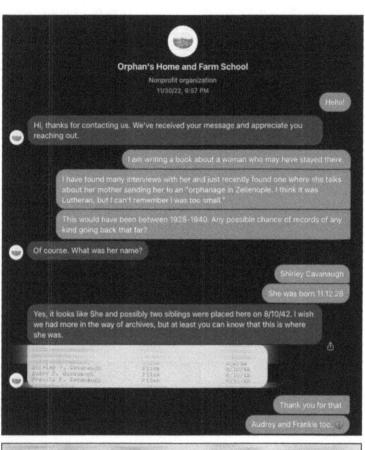

Orphan's Home and Farm School
Nonprofit organization
11/30/22, 9:57 PM

Hello!

Hi, thanks for contacting us. We've received your message and appreciate you reaching out.

I am writing a book about a woman who may have stayed there.

I have found many interviews with her and just recently found one where she talks about her mother sending her to an "orphanage in Zelienople. I think it was Lutheran, but I can't remember I was too small."

This would have been between 1928-1940. Any possible chance of records of any kind going back that far?

Of course. What was her name?

Shirley Cavanaugh

She was born 11.12.28

Yes, it looks like She and possibly two siblings were placed here on 8/10/42. I wish we had more in the way of archives, but at least you can know that this is where she was.

Thank you for that

Audrey and Frankie too.

Shirley V. Cavanaugh	Files	8/10/42
Audry R. Cavanaugh	Files	8/10/42
Francis F. Cavanaugh	Files	8/10/42

[1]

[1] Orphan's Home and Farm School, Facebook Messenger conversation, provided scans of records.

[2] Ferguson, Marilyn. "Shirley's Own Story: Tells of Her Early Life Spent In Numerous Welfare Homes." *Pittsburgh Sun-Telegraph*, 3 Mar. 1957, P. 1, Col 1. https://www.newspapers.com/image/524003125.

[3] Obituary for Francis F. Cavanaugh, 27 May, 1944, *Ancestry.com.*

[4] "Gumbert School." Sites.rootsweb.com, sites.rootsweb.com/~paallent/page17/page17.html.

[5] "Home of the Good Shepherd." Www.info-Ren.org, www.info-ren.org/projects/btul/Pennsylvania/pastaff/ai/HGS.html.

[6] "Western Center." Wikipedia, 10 Oct. 2023, wikipedia.org/wiki/Western_Center.

[7] Cavanaugh, Francis Floyd. U.S., Department of Veterans Affairs BIRLS Death File, 1850-2010. *Ancestry.com.*

[8] Lauterbach, Walter. Allegheny County Veterans Services, Veterans Grave Registration List, Pennsylvania, U.S., Veterans Burial Cards, 1777-2012. *Ancestry.com.*

Marriage to Walter Lauterbach

"I don't remember how old I was, 20 or 21, when I met him," Shirley said. "He was working for Westinghouse and making pretty good money. I only knew him a couple of months when we were married." [1]

Walter Lauterbach & Shirley Cavanaugh/Lauterbach

[Shirley's personal collection]

On April 21st, 1950, Shirley Cavanaugh and Walter Lauterbach were officially wed and for Shirley:

> "It was the most contented time in my existence.
> It was peaceful anyway." [1] [2]

Shirley even had aspirations of becoming an archeologist:

> "Every now and then I'd read in the paper where
> they dug up something old, and I always was
> fascinated by those things ... I wondered what
> life was like in those days." [1]

On March 30th, 1951, Shirley and Walter had a daughter and named her Judy Louise.

Then, approximately one month later, on May 1st, 1951, Walter, like most men his age at that time, enlisted in the Korean War. [3]

20

Out to sea, sailing for a fight, Walter was in the middle of the Pacific Ocean when he was summoned back home; an emergency unheard of had occurred: infant Judy had been abandoned. The landlord of Shirley's apartment found Judy and took her to the hospital.

The hospital contacted The Red Cross, who contacted the Lauterbachs and The Navy, who then recalled Walter back to Pittsburgh.

When Walter arrived home, he found his daughter but not his wife.

Shirley — was gone.

Leaving infant Judy alone, malnourished, dehydrated, and ill.[7]

Whatever the unseen circumstances may have been, Shirley abandoned everything she knew as familiar and went off in search of a new life …

While it is absolutely fair for Shirley and her actions to be resented by the Lauterbachs, what else could have been expected of her?

Shirley was born into *The* Depression and lived a life informed by scarcity, pollution, and trauma. By age 12, her abusive father had disappeared. At 14, her mother placed her in an orphanage. Later she returned "home" to the cramped house of an abusive stepfather and his family. Her father died. Her mother had her placed in the State Training School at Morganza. When Shirley

---

[7] And apparently drugged. In a 1996 interview, Judy was quoted as saying, "I was told that, before the age of 1, I was sent to the hospital to have my stomach pumped because Shirley would feed me paregoric, a narcotic, so I would sleep."

turned 20, her brother Francis left for the Army, and she left her family's "home" in search of peace.

Peace that she found by marrying Walter.

Peace she found taken from her one year later for the purposes of foreign warfare.

Walter was gone.

Everybody was gone.

Shirley, a person whose experience of life had been informed and guided by violence, abandonment, and poverty, acted in accord with only what she knew, and left Judy and Walter behind.

[1] Ferguson, Marilyn. "Shirley's Own Story: Tells of Her Early Life Spent In Numerous Welfare Homes." *Pittsburgh Sun-Telegraph*, 3 Mar. 1957, P. 1, Col 1. https://www.newspapers.com/image/524003125.

[2] Pennsylvania, U.S., Marriages, 1852-1968 *iMarriage Records/i. iPennsylvania Marriages./Various County Register of Wills Offices, Pennsylvania. 2016 Ancestry.com.*

[3] Pennsylvania, U.S., Veterans Burial Cards, 1777-2012 for Walter G Lauterbach Series 4 (Cards and Lists from Revolutionary War to 2012) Carton 19. *Ancestry.com.*

A Night Off at The Hollywood Show Bar

In 1953, Shirley made her attempt at a fresh start, working as a waitress in the canteen of The Carrie Furnace (an industrial blast furnace that specialized in the production of iron), located along the Monongahela River in Swissvale, Pennsylvania, a borough sharing a border with Braddock, where Shirley was born. Her new life included another attempt at motherhood. On Friday the 13th of November, 1953, Shirley gave birth to her second child. [1]

She named her Ruth.

And while Shirley and Walter were still (supposedly) seeing each other — Walter was not Ruth's father.

It was, however, on February 4th, 1954, when Shirley and Walter had a date planned at The Hollywood Show Bar in East Pittsburgh, that these mystery trysts came to an end. As Shirley sat waiting, for whatever reason, Walter was a no-show. [1] [2] [3]

Shirley was stood-up.

Abandoned — again.

Frustrated, Shirley went back to Walter's mom's house to end their relationship for good.

Shirley noticed upon returning that the house was dark and "crawled through a cellar window, rather than wake them" and took what few possessions of hers that remained there:

> ➤ An Argus camera, with flash unit and case
> ➤ A picture of Walter
> ➤ A picture of her daughter Judy
> ➤ Two books and her butterfly ring

24

The next morning, Walter found Shirley — not to apologize or explain his absence the night before, but rather to let Shirley know "Mom is pretty mad." [3]

Martha, Shirley's ex-mother-in-law, filed charges against Shirley for burglary. [4]

O & T 779

No. 42 _March_ Term, 1954

Commonwealth of Pennsylvania
vs.

Shirley Cavanaugh also known
as Shirley Lauterbach

Charge_ Burglary

Date of Information_ February 5th 195

On Oath of Mrs. Martha Lauterbach

BX 1123

Squire's Docket No. 1186

Coram
Frederick N. Megahan
Justice of the Peace
714 Ross Ave. Wilkinsburg, Pa.

COST PAID
3/5/56

Costs $

Pros. Priv. Counsel

Deft's Counsel

Bondsman

Address
7071 Penn St. N. Braddock, Pa.
Deft. Residence

Arrested at_ Rankin, Pa.

Officer_Jack Gallagher

714 Ross Ave. Wilkinsburg, Pa.

Pros. Found 718 Ardmore Blvd.
Wilkinsburg, Pa.

P. O. Naly Co., Law Blank Publishers, 415 Grant St., Pgh. 19, Pa.

[4]

[1] "Judge Studies Shirley's Bid For Freedom," *Pittsburgh Post-Gazette*, 8 Mar. 1957, P. 1, Col. 2 & P. 6 Col 2. https://www.newspapers.com/image/89450728.

[2] "Slusser to Prosecute Shirley." *The Pittsburgh Press*, 8 Mar. 1957, P. 1, Col. 8. https://www.newspapers.com/image/148064909.

[3] "Shirley Waiting for Her Release: 'Bad Police Must Pay'." *Pittsburgh Sun-Telegraph*, 8 Mar. 1957, P. 3, Col. 1. https://www.newspapers.com/image/524003358.

[4] Commonwealth of Pennsylvania vs. Shirley Cavanaugh, Charge of Burglary, O and T No. 42, Term March 1954, Date of Information February 5, 1954. On Oath of Martha Lauterbach.

The Burglary

On February 15th, 1954, Shirley was arrested by officer Jack Gallagher and brought to the county jail on the charge of burglary. [1]

On April 14th, 1954, a court-appointed behavioral specialist was requested by the District Attorney to provide an analysis of Shirley for her court date.

Through a thick lens of outdated psychological language and the patriarchal male dominator gaze, Dr. R.H. Kiefer provided his assessment of Shirley to the court:

➢ "The subject was not provided a normal home situation and has poor developmental history."
➢ "Incorrigible from a young age."
➢ "Sexually promiscuous and confined to Gumbert, Home of the Good Shepherd and later, Morganza."
➢ "The subject and her husband had considerable marital difficulty, she blames the mother-in-law and her husband's close attachment to her."
➢ "She then purposefully became impregnated by another man and gave birth to a girl at the Braddock General hospital in Nov of 1953."
➢ "Unpredictable behavior. She gives vent to her needs of the moment without consideration of others."
➢ "Her maternal instinct is not normal and she is incapable of deep seated emotional attachments."
➢ "The subject is irresponsible. Immature person. Quite egocentric. Who best fits into the category of a psychopathic personality."
➢ "She will probably continue to be a source of trouble.[8]" [2]

---

[8] And yet, somehow, all I can think is: fuck the patriarchy.

Shirley was brought before the court of Judge Harry M. Montgomery and, *without* counsel, entered a plea of guilty.[9] On April 26th, 1954, about two months *after* her arrest, she was released from county jail with three years of probation. [4]

---

[9] The well-known "Miranda Rights" were not in existence until the outcome of Miranda v. Arizona on June 13th, 1966, and weren't implemented into law until 1968. [3]

Shirley Cavanaugh Mugshot

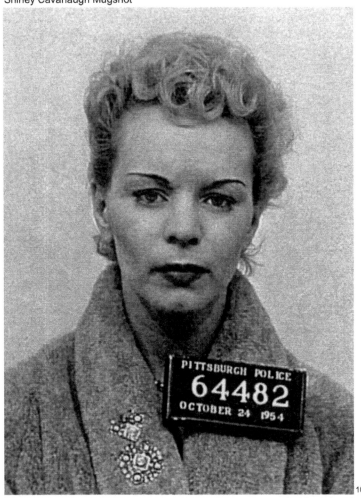

---

[10] I was not able to reconcile the date on her mugshot being eight months after her arrest in February. When I asked attorney Brandon Keller eabout this, his best guess was, "Shirley maybe was picked up on a probation violation. Probation is a mess and may not have been well documented back then. I can't think of any other reason. They take mugshots at the time of arraignment/bail."

Shirley Cavanaugh Mugshot

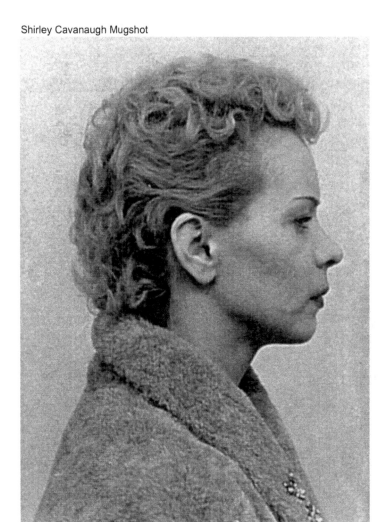

[Public domain]

April 14, 1954

TO: The Presiding Judge of Quarter Sessions Court

FROM: The Behavior Clinic

SUBJECT: SHIRLEY CAVANAUGH (LAUTENBACH), white female,
Catholic, divorced, cashier and counter-girl.
Address: 127 Park Way, East Pittsburgh, Pa.
#8562. Charge: Burglary.
Examined: February 1954.

REASON FOR REPORT: Requested by District Attorney.

S U M M A R Y

This subject was conceived prior to the marriage
of her parents, who were later separated and then divorced.
The mother has since remarried. The subject was not provided
with a normal home situation and has a poor developmental
history. She became known to Juvenile Court at an early age
as incorrigible. She refused to attend school and failed
many subjects because of lack of application. She became
sexually promiscuous and was confined at Gumbert School,
the Home of the Good Shepherd and later Morganza.

The subject and her husband have had considerable
marital difficulty, which she blames on the mother-in-law
and husband's close attachment to her. This finally led to a
divorce and the husband was awarded custody of the child.
She then purposely became impregnated by another man and gave
birth to a girl at the Braddock General Hospital in November
1953. She left the hospital against medical advice.

The whole history of this subject indicates
impulsive, unpredictable behavior, an alogical type of
reasoning and a wilful type of personality. She gives
vent to her needs of the moment without consideration of
others. Her maternal instinct is not normal and she is
incapable of deep seated emotional attachments. The
alleged offense was probably an unconscious revenge motive
against the mother-in-law, who filed the charge.

Our examination leads us to the impression that
the subject is an irresponsible, immature person, quite
egocentric and who best fits into the category of a
Psychopathic Personality. She will probably continue to
be a source of trouble.

Respectfully submitted,

R. H. Kiefer, M. D.

RHK:W

[2]

32

[1] Commonwealth of Pennsylvania vs. Shirley Cavanaugh, Charge of Burglary, O and T No. 42, Term March 1954, Date of Information February 5, 1954. On Oath of Martha Lauterbach.

[2] R.H. Kiefer, M. D. "Shirley Cavanaugh (Lauterbach): Analysis." The Behavior Clinic, 636 County Office Building, April 14, 1954.

[3] http://www.mirandawarning.org/historyofmirandawarning.

[4] Commonwealth of Pennsylvania vs. Shirley Cavanaugh, Probation No. 59265 No. 42 March Sessions, 1954. Probation by Order of Judge Montgomery.

Eugene Coon
(... *he forgot to duck ...*)

He Met Her in Downtown Club

Cop Calling Wagon, Girl 'Crowns' Him

A city policeman is nursing a "split" head today and a young divorcee is cooling her heels in jail as the result of a chance meeting early yesterday in a downtown club.

The cop, Eugene Coon, 26, assigned to the Squirrel Hill Police Station, needed two stitches in his head to repair the gash caused by a flying water glass.

The divorcee, Shirley Cavanaugh, 26, of 815 Federal St., was held over by Magistrate William Redmond on an aggravated assault charge at the request of Coon.

Coon testified that Shirley tossed the glass at him when he attempted to use the phone in her apartment to call a wagon.

He told Redmond he met Shirley in a Downtown club, but didn't identify the club.

Shirley said she is unemployed and lives alone. In asking the magistrate to hold the case over, Coon said:

"We are not prepared for this case yet. We have only signed information against her for aggravated assault."

In the meantime, the details of why Coon was the victim of a flying glass still remains a mystery.

Woman Dies of Burns

LOGAN, Feb. 12.—(AP.)— Mrs. Delnetta Gullett, 85, of Route 1, Delbarton, died in Holden Hospital today of burns suffered at the home of a daughter, Mrs. Kennis McCoy, last night.

SHIRLEY CAVANAUGH
... she tossed a glass ...
Sun-Telegraph Photo.

EUGENE COON
... he forgot to duck ...
Sun-Telegraph Photo.

Roughly one year later, on February 13th, 1955, an article appeared in the *Pittsburgh Sun-Telegraph* with the headline "Cop Calling Wagon, Girl 'Crowns' Him," where an awkward photo of Officer Eugene Coon appeared alongside a photo of Shirley Cavanaugh.

According to the article, Eugene and Shirley had a "chance meeting in a downtown club" and "Shirley tossed a glass at him when he attempted to use the phone in her apartment to call a wagon." How Coon came to be inside her apartment and why he was "the victim of a flying glass," the article concluded, "remains a mystery." [1]

He received two stitches in his head. [1]

The encounter became less mysterious, however, on March 10th, 1955, when the *Pittsburgh Sun-Telegraph* published the article, "Morals Charge Holds Woman" and it was revealed that *at least one* other time Coon had an identical "chance" meeting. [2]

34

"In front of a Downtown hotel" this time.

Coon met a woman named Corinne Miller, traveled back to her home with her, and offered her money — in exchange for sex. [2]

When she accepted, Coon arrested her, too.

On February 12th, 1955, Shirley Cavanaugh was arrested on charges of aggravated assault and battery of a police officer, and prostitution and assignation. [3]

Shirley Cavanaugh was a sex worker.

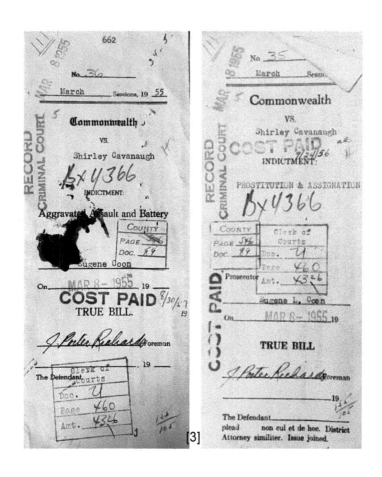

MAR 8 1955

662

No. 36

March _____ Sessions, 19 55

Commonwealth

VS.

Shirley Cavanaugh

Bx4366

INDICTMENT:

Aggravated Assault and Battery

COUNTY	
PAGE	
DOC.	89

Eugene Coon

On MAR 8- 1955 19 ____

COST PAID 8/30/57

TRUE BILL.

J. Peter Richards Foreman

_____ 19 ____

The Defendant Clerk of Courts

Doc.	4
Page	460
Amt.	4326

[3]

MAR 8 1955

No. 35

March _____ Sessi...

Commonwealth

VS.

Shirley Cavanaugh

COST PAID 9/24/56

INDICTMENT:

PROSTITUTION & ASSIGNATION

Bx4366

COUNTY	Clerk of Courts	
PAGE 546	Doc.	4
DOC. 89	Page	460
Prosecutor	Amt.	4326

Eugene L. Coon

On MAR 8- 1955 19

TRUE BILL

J. Peter Richards Foreman

_____ 19 ____

The Defendant _____

plead non cul et de hoc. District Attorney similiter. Issue joined.

INFORMATION.

N. B.   IN Filling OUT this BLANK, follow the words of the ACT of ASSEMBLY Strictly.

Commonwealth of Pennsylvania

vs.

Shirley Cavanaugh

COUNTY OF ALLEGHENY   ss.

Before me, the subscriber, a committing magistrate in and for the COUNTY OF ALLEGHENY, personally came   Eugene Coon

who, upon   his oath

duly administered according to law, deposes and says that at   Pittsburgh   in the COUNTY OF ALLEGHENY, on the   12th   day of   February   A. D. 195 5 defendant   aforesaid did then and there   offer and use the body of her, the said Shirley Cavanaugh for sexual intercourse for hire and in manner and form aforesaid unlawfully did then and there commit prostitution.

And that at Pittsburgh in the COUNTY OF ALLEGHENY on the 12th day of February defendant aforesaid did then and there unlawfully keep and use a certain building situated at 815 Federal Street in the City of Pittsburgh, County aforesaid for the purpose of prostitution and assignation.

And that at Pittsburgh in the COUNTY OF ALLEGHENY on the 12th day of February, A. D. 1955 did unlawfully, violently and maliciously commit an aggravated assault and battery upon the person of one, Eugene Coon, a police officer by hitting him with a glass in the face without just cause or provocation.

all of which is contrary to an Act of Assembly in such cases made and provided.

Complainant therefore prays and desires that a warrant may issue, and that defendant   may be arrested and held to answer this charge of Keeping Assignation House, Prostitution and and further deponent   saith not. Aggravated Assault and Battery.

Sworn to and subscribed before me, this

12th   day of

February,   A. D. 19 55

William Richman (SEAL)
Police Magistrate.

Eugene L. Coon

[4]

[1] "He Met Her in Downtown Club: Cop Calling Wagon, Girl 'Crowns' Him." *Pittsburgh Sun-Telegraph*, 13 Feb. 1955, P. 18, Col. 1. https://www.newspapers.com/image/524212995.

[2] "Morals Charge Holds Woman." *Pittsburgh Sun-Telegraph*, 10 Mar. 1955, P. 4, Col. 4. https://www.newspapers.com/image/524204694.

[3] Commonwealth of Pennsylvania vs. Shirley Cavanaugh, Charge of Aggravated Assault and Battery, Prostitution and Assignation. O and T No. 35 and No. 36, Date of Information March 8, 1955. On Oath of Eugene Coon.

[4] Commonwealth of Pennsylvania vs. Shirley Cavanaugh, Charge of Keeping Assignation House, Prostitution. Aggravated Assault and Battery. O and T No. 34, 35, 36. Term March 1955, Date of Information February 12, 1955 on Oath of Eugene L. Coon. *Allegheny County Records Dept.*

From the Furnace, with Love

In the March 3rd, 1957, *Pittsburgh Sun-Telegraph* article "Shirley's Own Story," she explained this situation further:

> "I worked in the Canteen of a mill in Rankin until three weeks before my little girl was born.[11] I told the hospital they'd have to sign a release for me to take my baby out the next afternoon. I didn't have money to pay hospitals. They let me go with her. She was sick. They told me she had leukemia and she'd have to go back into the hospital. I worked and saved money and she was in for five weeks.[12] They cured her.
>
> When I went back to work a week later, the baby's formula alone was costing me $1.90 a day.[13] I didn't have money to eat. This man kept coming and telling me he knew [a brothel] where I could make good money. Finally I agreed. It was three weeks before I could stand the idea of doing anything like that."

During her first night there:

> "County police raided it. The 'hostess' of the party called a Pittsburgh police official and after asking to 'fix' things for her, she tore up the warrant in the faces of the raiding officers. They left. [They were] paid to protect the house from such raids ... After another month, I went out on my own. But I still couldn't be like them. I kept trying to get

---

[11] This would be October 23rd, 1953.

[12] Records indicate two weeks. November 27th, 1953 - December 13th, 1953. [4]

[13] Inflation calculator: $1.90 in 1953 = $21.67 in 2023.

away from it. I even tried signing up to take courses in business school." [1] [2]

In February of 1955, after being arrested by Eugene Coon, Shirley was labeled as both burglar *and* aggressive prostitute. She sat alone at the age of 27, vulnerable in the Central Police Station without a support network to call upon.

In that moment of raw exposure — entered Acting Lieutenant Allen Carnahan, the head of Pittsburgh's Vice and Narcotic Squad.

He *immediately* recognized her worth and, in his own words, went on to "use Shirley as a stool pigeon"[14] until, as he stated it, "I saw she had outworn her usefulness." [3]

---

[14] "An informer who is sent into a group to report (as to the police) on its activities." [5]

IN THE

Court of Quarter Sessions of the Peace

FOR THE COUNTY OF ALLEGHENY

of March   Sessions, A. D. 19 55

Allegheny County, ss.

The Grand Inquest of the Commonwealth of Pennsylvania, now inquiring in and for the body of the County of Allegheny, upon their oaths and solemn affirmations, respectively, DO PRESENT, That

Shirley Cavanaugh

late of the County aforesaid   on the twelfth day of February , . in the year of our Lord one thousand nine hundred and **fifty-five** at the County aforesaid and within the jurisdiction of this Court, unlawfully did then and there offer and use the body of her the said Shirley Cavanaugh for sexual intercourse for hire and in manner and form aforesaid did then and there unlawfully commit prostitution and assignation.

contrary to the form of the Act of the General Assembly in such case made and provided and against the peace and dignity of the Commonwealth of Pennsylvania.

TRUE BIO RETURN.
~~Shirley Cavanaugh~~
Eugene Coon
O. Carnahan

James T. Malone, Jr.
District Attorney for Allegheny County

Sworn by me,

J Porter Richards
FOREMAN

[6]

[1] Ferguson, Marilyn. "Shirley Tells of Night...'" *Pittsburgh Sun-Telegraph*, 29 Oct. 1958, P. 3, Col. 1. https://www.newspapers.com/image/524526048.

[2] Ferguson, Marilyn. "Shirley's Own Story: Tells of Her Early Life Spent In Numerous Welfare Homes." *Pittsburgh Sun-Telegraph*, 3 Mar. 1957, P. 1, Col 1. https://www.newspapers.com/image/524003125.

[3] "Shirley Mum at Cop Trial: Carnahan Denies 'Affair'." *Pittsburgh Sun-Telegraph*, 31 May 1957, P. 1, Col. 8. https://www.newspapers.com/image/524012300.

[4] Dr. Lowrie M.D. Medical/Surgical Notes for Ruth Alma Cavanaugh. Braddock General Hospital. Admitted Nov. 27th, 1953, discharged Dec. 13th, 1953.

[5] "Stool pigeon." Merriam-Webster.com Dictionary, Merriam-Webster, https://www.merriam-webster.com/dictionary/stool%20pigeon.

[6] Commonwealth of Pennsylvania vs. Shirley Cavanaugh, Charge of Keeping Assignation House, Prostitution. Aggravated Assault and Battery. O and T No. 34, 35, 36. Term March 1955, Date of Information February 12, 1955 on Oath of Eugene L. Coon. Allegheny County Records Dept.

The Rockiest of Love Affairs

Shirley Cavanaugh & Allen Carnahan

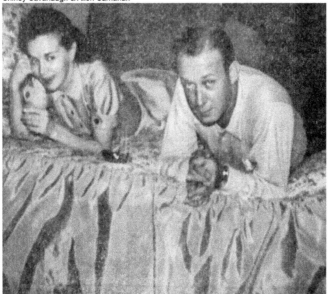

[Shirley's personal collection]

In 1955, Shirley Cavanaugh and Allen Carnahan began a relationship that lasted for several years. A relationship that, in modern times, would be labeled as extremely toxic. In 1955, however, Shirley labeled it as "the rockiest of love affairs." [1][2]

Through the years, they took frequent, out-of-town trips together to places where Carnahan was on assignment. Sharing flights and, naturally, hotel rooms. [1] In December of 1956, Carnahan attended the Federal Bureau of Narcotics' school in Washington, and while he was achieving perfect marks, Shirley was content and quiet ... in his hotel room. [2]

As the years passed, their relationship grew into a more complex, complicated situation: Allen had been married for more than two decades and was the father of two children; Shirley was his "stool pigeon" and she was in love. Carnahan began to drink

43

more regularly and more heavily. Coupled with his jealousy and aggressiveness, Shirley would often find herself "taking a punch in the mouth." [2][3]

And, as their relationship turned from rocky to toxic, then, ultimately, to life-threatening, there were no more out-of-town trips, no more hotel rooms, and no more flights.

There was only — a phone call.

On Sunday February 24th, 1957, at approximately 5 a.m., the head of the Pittsburgh Vice and Narcotic Squad, Acting Lieutenant Allen Carnahan, entered the Athletic Boosters Association (ABA) at 136 6th St. and, drunk, called the woman who loved him, his "useful stool pigeon," Shirley Cavanaugh, from the payphone.

> "Allen called me and told me to meet him at the ABA club real fast."

Carnahan made it clear that her presence in that bar, at that moment, was not a request.

> "He demanded I show up."

Shirley arrived at The ABA at approximately 5:15 a.m., where she and Allen immediately began to argue.

> "When I got to the club we argued ... He was in a drunken stupor."

At the bar, in a drunken lovers' fight, Allen reached toward his .38 special service revolver.

> "Like he has done in the past when he gets to drinking, he pulled his gun out and said, "I'm going to kill you and

myself. Here's the gun. You're afraid to shoot me."
[1][3][4][5]

As Carnahan pulled his gun from its holster, Shirley, terrified, slapped his hand away before he could aim at her.

The revolver — *BANG* — discharged, sending a .38 caliber bullet through Carnahan's right thigh, his groin, and ultimately lodging in his left thigh. Carnahan collapsed forward and fell into Shirley, knocking both of them to the barroom floor.

Noticing neither the blood stains on her clothes, nor the timely arrival of Lt. Francis Walsh, Shirley stood and yelled:

"Did I shoot you? Allen? Are you hurt?!" [6]

Shirley, gripped by panic, asked bar patron Joseph L. Rosso, a truck driver, to take her home. In shock himself, Joseph agreed, and the two of them disappeared down the stairs and out the front entrance. [6]

Carnahan lay bleeding on the barroom floor when he noticed Lt. Walsh.

"Get me to a hospital," Carnahan screamed in agony. "I shot myself!"

The ABA's entire crowd panicked and split for the door. [6]

[1] "Shirley's Love Letters Confiscated by Police: Her Apartment Ransacked." *The Pittsburgh Press*, 28 Feb. 1957, P. 1, Col. 2. https://www.newspapers.com/image/148011130.

[2] "Carnahan Apt U.S. Pupil: He Learned to Detect Vice With Shirley." *Pittsburgh Post-Gazette*, 5 Mar. 1957, P. 11, Col. 1. https://www.newspapers.com/image/89450642.

[3] Knezevich, Nicholas. "Woman Says Cop Was Shot by Accident in Love Affair: She Gives Up, Changes Story; Out on Bond." *The Pittsburgh Press*, 27 Feb. 1957, P.1, Col. 4-8. https://www.newspapers.com/image/148007997.

[4] "Shirley in Jail, Blames Carnahan." *Pittsburgh Sun-Telegraph*, 2 Mar. 1957, P. 1, Col. 6. https://www.newspapers.com/image/524003104.

[5] "Judge Revokes Call-Girl's Probation: Shirley Sentenced to Muncy." *Pittsburgh Post-Gazette*, 2 Mar. 1957, P. 1, Col. 4-5. https://www.newspapers.com/image/89450576.

[6] "Carnahan Faces Trial Board." *The Pittsburgh Press*, 5 Mar. 1957, P.4, Col. 1. https://www.newspapers.com/image/148057906.

"Will I know your name or recognise your face?
Or by what means I'll be delivered from this place?
Here comes the gun, there goes the flash
once the bullet leaves it's never coming back."

David Sylvian, from "The Scent of Magnolia"

The Carnahan Affair
Monday, February 25th, 1957

The *Pittsburgh Post-Gazette*, the *Record-Argus*, the *Daily American*, and the *Pittsburgh Sun-Telegraph* all reported identical details. Carnahan was "working on something," the shot was a "self-inflicted accident," and Carnahan was "recovering in Allegheny General Hospital" where all the doctors reported his condition was "satisfactory." [1][2][3][4]

The only thing was, there were witnesses and, what's more, Carnahan couldn't, in any way, keep his story straight. Almost overnight, there were three versions he told:

1. He was moving his revolver from his left coat pocket to his right hip holster. In the process, his pistol discharged, sending a bullet into his left thigh. [1][2][3][4]
2. Carnahan retracted this original statement, explaining he was "in shock when he made [it]" and that a woman named Shirley Cavanaugh, a woman he said had recently been "bothering" him, came up behind him when he sat at the bar and "pulled out his revolver and shot him." Carnahan said he knew of "no reason why she would shoot him." [5] [6] [7]
3. Retracting both the previous stories, Carnahan claimed he was walking past the bar, when a woman who he didn't know stopped him, impulsively started an argument, took his revolver from its holster, and shot him in the groin. [8]

The aggregate of these contradictions were seen clearly for what they were: an attempted coverup.

A coverup that may have succeeded, had it not been for the Director of Public Safety, Judge Louis Rosenberg.

[1] "Lt. Carnahan is Accidentally Shot by Own Revolver." *Daily American*, 25 Feb. 1957, P. 7, Col. 7. https://www.newspapers.com/image/511094283.

[2] "Lt. Carnahan Wounds Self: Own Gun Goes Off." *Pittsburgh Sun-Telegraph*, 25 Feb. 1957, P. 13, Col. 9, https://www.newspapers.com/image/524002899.

[3] "Pennsylvania News Briefs." *Record-Argus*, 25 Feb. 1957, P. 12, Col. 5. https://www.newspapers.com/image/10926009.

[4] "Cop Shot With Own Gun." *Pittsburgh Post-Gazette*, 25 Feb. 1957, P. 1, Col. 2. https://www.newspapers.com/image/90017904.

[5] "Detective Admits Woman Shot Him." *Altoona Tribune*, 26 Feb. 1957, P. 2, Col. 8. https://www.newspapers.com/image/58076361.

[6] "Divorcee Hunted in Cop's Shooting." *Pittsburgh Sun-Telegraph*, 26 Feb. 1957, P.1, Col. 3. https://www.newspapers.com/image/524002922.

[7] "Police Seek Divorcee: Woman Accused of Shooting Pittsburgh Officer." *The York Dispatch*, 27 Feb. 1957, P. 9, Col. 3. https://www.newspapers.com/image/614370919.

[8] "Officer Now Admits Woman Wounded Him." *The Pittsburgh Press,* 26 Feb. 1957, P. 1, Col. 5. https://www.newspapers.com/image/148005328.

Louis Rosenberg

Educated at Duquesne University School of Law in 1923, Rosenberg built for himself an impressive resumé: Special Counsel for Allegheny County Emergency Relief in 1935; Special Deputy Attorney General of the Commonwealth of Pennsylvania from 1936 to 1939; Special Counsel for the Commonwealth of Pennsylvania from 1939 to 1941; Special Assistant City Solicitor for the City of Pittsburgh from 1941 to 1956.

[Wiki Commons Image]

And from 1956 to 1961, Louis Rosenberg was the Director of Public Safety for the City of Pittsburgh, during which time he took control of what became known as "The Carnahan Affair." [1]

Rosenberg, without any apparent bias, placed himself as the figurehead in resolving this case. A case involving one of the highest-ranking officers on the Pittsburgh Police force and a 28-year-old sex worker with a previous record of burglary, assault and battery of a police officer, prostitution, and assignation. [2]

The immediacy of Rosenberg's response to this situation was impressive on many levels:

- February 24th, 1957, Sunday morning, the shot was fired.
- February 25th, 1957, Monday afternoon, Carnahan was recovering, a coverup was happening.
- February 26th, 1957, Tuesday morning, the papers read, "Director of Public Safety Louis Rosenberg demands 'all the facts' in this case."

50

In the *Post-Gazette* article "Woman Shot Dope Squad Boss: Carnahan Reverses First Story" Rosenberg was quoted as saying, "... we will do whatever the law tells us we must do as soon as we get all the facts in this case," stating there were "many varying reports" on what happened. "At first it appeared there were 20 persons in the club at the time, later I heard there were only six ..."

While it was reported that Superintendent of Police James W. Slusser planned, and began to implement, his own inquiry board, Rosenberg would not allow the police to investigate themselves.[15]

Rosenberg stated:

> "I will keep complete and absolute supervision of this affair. There will be no police involved except those called in for questioning. There is only one way to know what is right and that is to do it myself." [3]

In a February 28th, 1957 *Pittsburgh Press* article titled "After-Hours Clubs on Spot Over Shooting: Rosenberg Orders Check as Result of Carnahan Case," Rosenberg was quoted as saying:

> "While the superintendent of police is in active charge of the inquiry, I shall observe and act in accordance with my discretionary powers as head of the department. That is my power, to make and direct such inquiries as I see fit. I want the facts." [4]

Shirley got ahead of the situation by calling a journalist at The *Pittsburgh Press*. She denied she knew Carnahan, denied she'd ever heard of The ABA, and provided the alibi of playing cards at

---

[15] Smart move.

her mother's house. Ultimately, Shirley dropped this *fantastic* quote:

> "Me, have anything to do with a cop? Are you kidding? What would I be doing out with him at that time of the morning, or any time for that matter? I definitely don't like cops." [5]

Soon "Divorcee Hunted in Cop's Shooting" was sensationalized across the front page of the *Pittsburgh Sun-Telegraph* alongside Shirley's photograph. And, as the Pittsburgh Police began their search for Shirley, the public eye began to close in.

On Tuesday, February 26th, 1957, at precisely midnight, Shirley walked into the Penn Police Station to surrender.

She spoke only three lines:

"I'm Shirley."

"I'm not talking until I see my attorney."

And, when asked if she shot Carnahan, "I have nothing to say right now." [6][7]

Shirley Cavanaugh

[1] United States District Court Western District of Pennsylvania Home, Judges Western District of Pennsylvania, Louis Rosenberg. https://www.pawd.uscourts.gov/louis-rosenberg.

[2] Commonwealth of Pennsylvania vs. Shirley Cavanaugh, Charge of Keeping Assignation House, Prostitution. Aggravated Assault and Battery. O and T No. 34, 35, 36. Term March 1955, Date of Information February 12, 1955 on Oath of Eugene L. Coon.

[3] "Parole Violation Jails Shirley." *The Pittsburgh Press*, 1 Mar. 1957, P. 1, Col. 7.
https://www.newspapers.com/image/148005328.

[4] "After-Hours Clubs on Spot Over Shooting: Rosenberg Orders Check as Result of Carnahan Case." *The Pittsburgh Press*, 28 Feb. 1957, P. 2, Col. 1.
https://www.newspapers.com/image/148011130.

[5] "Woman Shot Dope Squad Boss: Carnahan Reverses First Story, All He Wanted in Club Was Java." *Pittsburgh Post-Gazette*, 26 Feb. 1957, P. 1, Col. 8.
https://www.newspapers.com/image/90018102.

[6] "Shoot Story Denied by Accused Woman: She Was With Another Man at Time, Press Reporter Told During Interview." *The Pittsburgh Press*, 26 Feb. 1957, P. 1, Col. 5.
https://www.newspapers.com/image/148005328.

[7] "Divorcee Hunted in Cop's Shooting." *Pittsburgh Sun-Telegraph*, 26 Feb. 1957, P.1, Col. 3.
https://www.newspapers.com/image/524002922.

Wednesday, February 27th, 1957[16]

Shirley was arraigned before Magistrate John Fiorucci and was held for court on $5,000 bond. She entered no plea at the preliminary hearing. [1] [2] Carnahan was suspended from the force and detective Howard Ingold took over as head of the Vice Squad. [3]

Shirley posted bail,[17] and returned home to find her apartment had been ransacked by police. Multiple items were missing, including:

➢ A chest full of love letters from acquaintances
➢ A scrapbook of clippings about the exploits of Lt. Carnahan
➢ A book of souvenirs (hotel and gift receipts, plane ticket stubs, and dated postcards) from their trips together
➢ An album of photographs, including some of Lt. Carnahan [4]

"He was my world ... though he may not have treated me nice I would never have harmed him ... I went to him for help after I was arrested several times, thinking it was better to know a cop well than to be running away from them all the time. I admit that I played up to him at first for kicks, but I got to see him so often that we began talking of marriage." [5]

Walter Geisey, the executive secretary to Mayor David L. Lawrence, mailed newspaper clippings to the mayor who, at the time, was touring West Germany.

---

[16] This date was sourced from the publication farthest from Pittsburgh to include coverage on Shirley's story: *Tulsa Daily World*, in an article entitled "Woman Sought After Officer Says She Used His Gun On Him."

[17] I was unable to uncover how this was paid.

This was not the only time Mayor Lawrence was going to hear about The Carnahan Affair.[18] [6]

---

[18] One of my favorite things about this was the speed of communication. The article "After-Hours Clubs on Spot Over Shooting: Rosenberg Orders Check as Result of Carnahan Case" stated, "Deputy Mayor Charles D. McCarthy, acting in the absence of Mayor David L. Lawrence said, 'Clippings of newspaper stories have been air-mailed to Mayor Lawrence. There has been no word back from him, but–since the mail takes about five days–it is unlikely that he has received them yet.'"

The Pittsburgh Press

FINAL

WOMAN SAYS COP WAS SHOT
BY ACCIDENT IN LOVE AFFAIR

Racket Probe Witness, Kin Threatened

Bootlegger Back on Stand

U.S. Builds Up Pressure on Israel Again

Get Out of Egypt, Dulles Says in Point-Blank Appeal

She Gives Up, Changes Story; Out on Bond

She Gives Up, Her Story; Posts Bond — An 'Accident'

24 Tankers Ends Spring Preview

Pittsburgh Post-Gazette

One of America's Great Newspapers

Final City Edition

WOMAN IN SHOOTING GIVES UP

Senate Probe Links Teamsters to Vice

Shady Deal In Politics Is Related

U.S. Drafts Middle-Way Israel Plan

High Rates Hurt Business, Industrialist Warns

Rockwell Raps State Taxes

Suspect Faces Cop Case Quiz

State, U.S. to Finance Crosstown Blvd. Here

Slash of Pike Truck Tolls Recommended

Pittsburgh Post-Gazette, Feb 27, 1957.

[19] During The Carnahan Affair, political cartoonist Cy Hungerford created 11 illustrations regarding The Carnahan Affair. For more information on the life and times of Cy Hungerford, look up the works of historian Terri Blanchette. The Ohio County Public Library hosted, and reposted, a livestream Q&A with Blanchette that was incredibly informative and entertaining. I couldn't recommend it more. [7]

[1] "Arrest Woman for Shooting Detective." *The News Herald,* Wed. Feb. 27, 1957, P.1, Col. 4. https://www.newspapers.com/image/57646949.

[2] "Girl Freed on Bond in Shooting." *The Evening Standard,* Thurs. Feb. 28 1957, P. 7, Col. 1. https://www.newspapers.com/image/27826365.

[3] "Wounded Cop Suspended From Force, Loved Carnahan, Woman Says." *Pittsburgh Post-Gazette.* Thurs. Feb. 28, 1957, P. 1, Col. 2, https://www.newspapers.com/image/90018496.

[4] "Shirley's Love Letters Confiscated by Police: Her Apartment Ransacked." *The Pittsburgh Press*, Thurs. Feb. 28 1957, P. 2, Col. 1. https://www.newspapers.com/image/148011130.

[5] "Woman Tells Story of Cop Shooting: Her Story: An Accident." *The Pittsburgh Press*, Wed. 27 Feb. 1957, P. 1, Col. 8. https://www.newspapers.com/image/148007997.

[6] "Mayor to Read About Shooting." *The Pittsburgh Press*, Wed. 27 Feb. 1957. P. 12, Col. 6. https://www.newspapers.com/image/148008753.

[7] LUNCH WITH BOOKS LIVESTREAM: Wheeling Presents: Lesser Known Legends of Wheeling - Cy Hungerford https://www.ohiocountylibrary.org/calendar/lunch-with-books-livestream-wheeling-presents-lesser-known-legends-of-wheeling---cy-hungerford/2457

Thursday, February 28th, 1957[20]

According to *The Pittsburgh Press* article "Cops Ignored Basic
Rules in Shooting Case: Police Regulations Not Followed in
'Investigation'," [1] there were four rules that police were trained
to follow in the wake of a shooting:

1. Top-ranking officer at the scene of the shooting must remain
   there until relieved.
2. All evidence must be guarded.
3. Witnesses should be asked their names and addresses, and
   statements taken from them. If felt trustworthy, they may be
   released to visit headquarters the next day to give
   statements.
4. Evidence should be carefully handled to preserve
   fingerprints.

The article proceeded to explain how each one of these
rudimentary steps was entirely ignored by the policemen trained
to enforce them:

1. Lt. Walsh, the top-ranking officer, who arrived at The ABA
   within seconds of hearing the gunshot,[21] called for an
   ambulance to take Carnahan to the hospital. Lt. Walsh then
   left the scene and rode, in the ambulance, with Carnahan to
   Allegheny General Hospital.
2. As there was no longer a police presence in the club, no
   evidence could have been guarded. The ABA became
   trampled by unmonitored guests and employees.
3. As there were no police present to contain the crowd, only
   one person was able to be positively identified as being in

---

[20] A *Post-Gazette* reporter caught an interview with Shirley's roommate,
a woman named Marie Linden. Linden claims Shirley came home drunk
at 6:00 a.m. and said, "I just shot Allen!" As the days moved forward,
some articles attempted to make a "Gotcha!" moment out of this, but it
doesn't pick up much traction. [2] [3]

[21] Sus.

the club at the time: Peter Kryimes, the club treasurer, who only had one thing to say: "I didn't see it."

4. In the event of a shooting, the gun was to either have been "left alone until fingerprint men arrive or lifted by inserting a pencil in the muzzle." In the case of Carnahan's gun, well, "the wounded officer's pistol, the weapon used in the shooting, evidently was picked off the floor by Lt. Walsh."

Pittsburgh Post-Gazette, February 28, 1957.

Too Hot to Hush Up

THE shooting of Police Lieutenant Allen Carnahan is significant not so much because a peace officer was shot—a matter of more than passing interest in itself—but because of the circumstances under which it occurred.

From the confused picture which has slowly emerged, we get the impression that a bunch of the boys—and girls—was whooping it up, much in the manner of the Malamute saloon, when out of the not-so-small hours of a Sunday morning came a woman whose name was trouble.

When the smoke of Officer Carnahan's pistol had cleared and the merrymakers had fled into a cheerless dawn, there began a clumsy official attempt to cover up for the fallen officer. It was all an accident, officials reported, and everything was going to be all right.

Unhappily for the police, the damning spots wouldn't out. Embarrassing questions were inherent in the whole affair. How come police officers—and allegedly there were several — were frequenting a private club which was violating the law by operating hours afer it should have been closed? Why didn't the officers question witnesses and arrest the woman who admits she was involved in the shooting? Why did police wait until newspapermen had found and questioned the woman before taking her into custody?

The answer is, of course, that the police dread a scandal within the fraternity and will go to stupid lengths in an attempt to hush it up. But that answer isn't good enough for the public. Better ones should result from an official investigation of the whole scandalous episode.

Pittsburgh Post Gazette Thursday, February 28, 1957

[1] "Cops Ignored Basic Rules in Shooting Case: Police Regulations Not Followed in 'Investigation'." The Pittsburgh Press, Thurs. Feb. 28 1957, P. 2, Col. 4. https://www.newspapers.com/image/148011130.

[2] "Shirley Drunk on Morning Cop Was Shot: Roommate Tells of Her Announcing 'I Just Shot Allen'." *Pittsburgh Post-Gazette.* Thurs. Feb. 28, 1957, P. 1, Col. 3, https://www.newspapers.com/image/90018496.

[3] "Says Shirley Confessed: Roommate Tells Shooting Story." *Pittsburgh Sun-Telegraph*, Thurs. Feb. 28 1957, P. 1, Col. 2. https://www.newspapers.com/image/524003033.

Friday, March 1st, 1957

Judge Harry M. Montgomery[22] called Shirley into court and asserted that a "burglary probationer [has] no business being in a club at 5 a.m. when legal closing hours are 3 a.m." He then ordered Shirley to be held in county jail until she could be properly sentenced. He insisted that Shirley then be sent to the State Industrial School at Muncy for an "indefinite" and "indeterminate" stay until she "regains some self-respect."[23] [1] [2]

As Shirley sat in county jail, waiting to be processed for Muncy, the clock ticked tensely.

Shirley's attorney, John Snee,[24] and Safety Director Rosenberg were losing time and began their official probe into the case. Over the next several days, Rosenberg would call a total of 39 witnesses, and Snee would embark on what he called the "Free Shirley" campaign. [3] [4]

Rosenberg began immediately, stating:

> "I am going into this thing in a patient manner like a lawyer. I am going to check it step-by-step, bit by bit. I am going to do this in a manner which will construct, not destroy."

---

[22] The same judge that gave Shirley three years' probation on April 26th, 1954 for her "burglary."

[23] Indeterminate/Indefinite sentences were legal sentencing lengths in all 50 states from 1930-1970s. [5]

[24] It is unclear how Snee and Shirley were put in touch with each other, nevertheless he remained her attorney throughout.

[Pittsburgh Sun Telegraph Friday Mar 1, 1957]

Along with Councilman David Olbum and First Assistant Pittsburgh Solicitor James Legnard, Rosenberg called his first witness: Lt. Walsh, the first officer on the scene. Rosenberg instructed Lt. Walsh to meet them at a closed ABA, where a porter waited to let them in.

Upon entry, Rosenberg wasted no time and demanded Walsh to recall, in detail, The ABA when he arrived on February 24th. Any time Walsh answered "along lines other than those [Rosenberg] opened with, Rosenberg would cut him off insisting, 'we'll get to that later.'" [6]

When asked how he happened to arrive at The ABA the moment he did, Walsh replied, "I was on my way to the Rock and Roll Club a few doors away in response to a call that someone had been locked in. As I was passing The ABA, I saw two men walk out and wondered why, since the club was supposed to be closed. I started up The ABA stairs to find out, that's when I heard the shot."[25] [6]

---

[25] Still sus.

SCENE OF COP SHOOTING—Standing around the low-backed bar stools where Lt. Allen Carnahan and call-girl Shirley Cavanough were sitting when he was shot are, left to right, City Safety Director Louis Rosenberg, Asst. City Solicitor James G. Legnard, Lt. Francis Walsh, and City Councilman David Olbum. They studied the scene of the shooting at the Athletic Boosters Club today.

[Pittsburgh Press Fri Mar 1, 1957]

A reporter from the *Pittsburgh Sun-Telegraph* caught up with Walsh after his 55-minute interview with Rosenberg to ask how it went.

Walsh could only reply, "It was rough ..." [6]

[1] "Parole Violation Jails Shirley." *The Pittsburgh Press*, 1 Mar. 1957, P. 1, Col. 7.
https://www.newspapers.com/image/148005328

[2] "Shirley Cheered as She Leaves Jail." *The Pittsburgh Press* Thurs. 14 Mar. 1957, P. 1, Col. 2.
https://www.newspapers.com/image/148076769

[3] "5 ½ Day Probe Ends: Draft Report on Police Shooting." The *Indiana Gazette* Fri. 8 Mar. 1957, P. 1, Col. 2.
https://www.newspapers.com/image/540597581

[4] "Promises Full 'Cover-Up' Story: 39 Questioned In Police Shooting Case." The *News-Herald* Fri. 8 Mar. 1957, P. 1, Col. 4.
https://www.newspapers.com/image/57647955

[5] https://en.wikipedia.org/wiki/Indefinite_imprisonment

[6] Bell, Ed. "Rosenberg Goes to Club to Get On Spot Story: Police Boss Probes Shooting of Cop." *Pittsburgh Sun-Telegraph*, Fri. 1 Mar. 1957, P.1, Col. 7.
https://www.newspapers.com/image/524003076

Saturday, March 2nd, 1957
Shirley in County Jail: Day One

Multiple newspapers from the *Pittsburgh Sun-Telegraph* to the *Pittsburgh Post-Gazette* and *The Pittsburgh Press* published photos of Shirley with her weeping face buried in a handkerchief.

These articles reinforced the idea that Shirley had violated her probation with headlines like "Shirley in Jail, Blames Carnahan" and "Shirley to Serve Indefinite Sentence." [1]

Across the articles, Shirley was consistently blamed for having "violated probation by leaving the court's jurisdiction on trips with Lieutenant Carnahan." [26]

Loudly and publicly, Snee called out Judge Montgomery by saying, "Probation revocation is a lousy trick," and announced that he intended to "seek a writ of habeas corpus on the grounds that she was not adequately represented at the burglary trial in 1954." [27] [1] [3]

Not wanting to set a precedent Judge Montgomery refused this request, stating:

---

[26] A quote from a March 16th, 1957 *Pittsburgh Post-Gazette* article, "Shirley Wins a Round," was incredibly appropriate for this blatant double standard: "There is no doubt that Shirley violated the terms of her parole. But neither is there any doubt that she had been violating them for a long time, with the knowledge if not with the connivance and at the pleasure of the police. So long as she was useful to them, the police were quite content with her infractions. How, then, can one avoid the feeling that the police have ill-used this girl?"

[27] Quietly and in private, during their regular meetings together, Shirley began to dictate a 22-page "tell-all" file regarding not only her relationship with the Pittsburgh Police Bureau, but also everything she knew about bribery and corruption within the police force. [2]

"If I *do* release her, every man in the Allegheny County Workhouse who thinks he has grounds for habeas corpus will come in for release on bail." [4]

Snee, however, still maintained that this was Shirley's clear path to freedom. If he successfully had Shirley's burglary conviction *nolle prossed*,[28] it would mean that, in 1954, Shirley should never have been placed on probation. Therefore, on February 24th, at The ABA, she could not have been in violation *of* that probation. As a result, Shirley's detainment, in 1957, would be illegal and the courts would be in violation of her civil liberties.

Snee quickened his pace and began his "Free Shirley" campaign by first making an official call for Shirley's 1954 court-appointed attorney, Charles B. Jarrett, to appear before the courts for examination.[29]

Meanwhile, Rosenberg's witnesses turned up and spilled the truth. He had already interviewed eight people, including police Superintendent Slusser and Assistant Superintendent Lawrence J. Maloney.[30] Slusser was reported as having walked out "smiling after more than two hours" and had no comment, whereas Maloney emerged after "one hour and 35 minutes," and simply remarked to a newsman that, "Somebody's going to get hurt ..." [5]

---

[28] A legal term from the Latin *nolle prosequi* meaning "to be unwilling to pursue."

[29] When a *Post-Gazette* journalist caught up with Jarrett, we learned that, shockingly, he "didn't do anything except stand there," and stated, "I didn't think it was a burglary." [1] [3]

[30] At that point, *The Pittsburgh Press* reported that Rosenberg's probe "may engulf the entire Pittsburgh Police Bureau." [5]

Councilman David Olbum stated, "We are looking into everything, including possible underworld payoffs for police protection," and Rosenberg declared his plan to quiz Carnahan "by his hospital bedside if I have to." Rosenberg continued:

"I will spare no one to get to the bottom of this. We hope to be able to come up with something. We want to make a report to the mayor as fast as possible. The findings also will be made known to the public. The people are entitled to know." [5]

Pittsburgh Post-Gazette, March 2, 1957.

Sunday's Sun-Telegraph Has the *NEW LOOK!*

Inside Today

MYSTERY NOVEL

The Voice of Death

Plus

BIG RECORD·TV·RADIO SECTIONS

Pittsburgh Sun·Telegraph

FINAL EDITION

Israel Cabinet Called

Bedside Quiz for Carnahan

Ben-Gurion Calls Cabinet Over Gaza

Missourian Chosen For Top Court

Beck to Face Quiz on Vote Fund Offer

Another Club on the Spot

Police Boss Hunts For Cover Up

The Pittsburgh Press

FINAL Latest Stocks

PAROLE VIOLATION JAILS SHIRLEY

Pinball Czar Denies Payoff To Union

Director Probes Shooting

Israel Sets Gaza, Aqaba Withdrawal

N. Y. Firm Gives Low Tunnel Bid

Safety Chief Takes Over In Cop Case

Stiff Zoning Rules Vetoed by Council

County Plans Flat Raise

Sleuth's Pals Offer Alibis

[1] "Shirley to Serve Indefinite Sentence: Woman Accused of Shooting Officer Arrested as Probation Violator." *The Pittsburgh Press.* Sat. 2 Mar. 1957, P. 1, Col. 5.
https://www.newspapers.com/image/148043980

[2] "Probe Hunts 'Payoffs' in Carnahan Affair, Carnahan Quiz May Engulf Entire Force." *The Pittsburgh Press.* Sat. 2 Mar. 1957, P. 1, Col. 7.
https://www.newspapers.com/image/148043980

[3] "Shirley Sentenced to Muncy: Court Told of Out-of-Town Trips She Made With Vice Squad Boss Who Was Shot in Sixth Ave. Club" *Pittsburgh Post-Gazette* Sat. Mar 2, 1957, P. 1, Col. 4.
https://www.newspapers.com/image/89450576

[4] "Shirley Fights Prison With DA on Her Side." *Pittsburgh Sun-Telegraph.* Thurs. Mar 7, 1957, P. 3, Col. 1.
https://www.newspapers.com/image/524003322

[5] "Bedside Quiz for Carnahan: Rosenberg to Quiz Carnahan, Shirley in shooting: Police Boss Hunts for Cover Up." *Pittsburgh Sun-Telegraph.* Sat. Mar 2, 1957, P. 1, Col. 7.
https://www.newspapers.com/image/524003104

Pittsburgh Sun Telegraph Sun Mar 3, 1957

In spring of 1957, the *Pittsburgh Sun-Telegraph* ran an article by Marilyn Ferguson entitled "Shirley's Own Story: Tells of Her Early Life Spent in Numerous Welfare Homes," in which, for the first time, Shirley's voice was heard and many intimate details regarding her traumatic life were shared. [1]

More witnesses were called by Rosenberg to give their statements, including The ABA's chef, waiter, bartender, owner, and hatcheck girl. [2]

Mayor David Lawrence received the newspaper clippings while in Germany and responded to the *Pittsburgh Sun-Telegraph* saying,

> "I am shocked to hear this. Lt. Carnahan is a very able young man." [3]

[1] Ferguson, Marilyn. "Shirley's Own Story: Tells of Her Early Life Spent In Numerous Welfare Homes." *Pittsburgh Sun-Telegraph*, 3 Mar. 1957, P. 1, Col 1.
https://www.newspapers.com/image/524003125

[2] "Hat Check Girl, Boss Sleuth In Shooting Quiz." *Pittsburgh Sun-Telegraph*, Sun. 3 March 1957, P. 8, Col. 1.
https://www.newspapers.com/image/524003132

[3] "Shooting Shocks Lawrence." *Pittsburgh Sun-Telegraph*, Sun. 3 March 1957, P. 8, Col. 7.
https://www.newspapers.com/image/524003132

Monday, March 4th, 1957
Shirley in County Jail: Day Three

The *Pittsburgh Post-Gazette* published the article "Shirley's 'Surrender' Proves to be Phony," in which it was reported that the police staged the whole thing. [1]

On Tuesday, February 26th, 1957, at 9 p.m., Shirley was arrested. She was taken to the Squirrel Hill Police Station, where she was then placed in the car of Assistant Police Superintendent Lawrence J. Maloney. She was driven around for three hours before she was finally dropped off at Penn Station to "surrender" at midnight. [1] [2]

Pittsburgh Post-Gazette, March 4, 1957.

Explained Maloney, "It is nothing unusual. We questioned her first at No. three police station and then rode around with her trying to get her to talk. She refused to make any statement." [1] [2]

At midnight, Shirley was dropped off at Penn Station and didn't say anything outside of "I'm Shirley," "I'm not talking until I see my attorney," and "I have nothing to say right now." [31]

At that point, neither Shirley nor Carnahan had given their statements to Rosenberg. Shirley's attorney, John Snee, reported to the press:

> "[I will] not permit questioning of my client unless the police get her out of jail. And I don't mean on a court order," he concluded, "I mean out of jail, period." [3]

Carnahan's attorney, Louis C. Glasso, reported that Carnahan had been running a fever and was scheduled for surgery to remove the bullet from his leg. As such, he remained in a state unfit for questioning. Glasso was expected to make a statement on his behalf the following day. [3]

---

[31] However much it would have been conjecture, it was possible that the journalist Shirley called at *The Pittsburgh Press* earlier that day may have informed her to say nothing until she had proper legal counsel (something which she had to learn the hard way with her 1954 burglary charge, where Shirley entered a plea of guilty without representation). I also often wonder if it was Marilyn Ferguson with whom she spoke.

[1] "Shirley's 'Surrender' Proves to be Phony." *Pittsburgh Post-Gazette,* Mon. Mar. 4, 1957, P. 1, Col. 1.
https://www.newspapers.com/image/89450600

[2] "Cop-Shooter Surrender was 'Staged'." *Indiana Gazette,* Mon. Mar. 4, 1957, P. 15, Col. 3.
https://www.newspapers.com/image/540597434

[3] "Shooting Probe Names Secret Eye-Witnesses: Rosenberg to Question Carnahan Today." *The Pittsburgh Press.* Mon. Mar. 4, 1957, P. 1, Col. 6.
https://www.newspapers.com/image/148055444

[4] "Mystery Witnesses in Police Inquiry." *Valley Independent,* Mon Mar 4, 1957, P.5, Col. 3.
https://www.newspapers.com/image/9696186

Tuesday, March 5th, 1957
Shirley in County Jail: Day Four

Much to everyone's surprise, Carnahan's attorney, Louis C. Glasso, reported:

> "Carnahan has agreed that Miss Cavanaugh's version was the correct one. The gun accidentally discharged while he and the girl were scuffling. Carnahan will not be pressing charges against Shirley and states he will 'refuse to testify against her even if someone else files charges.'" [1] [2] [3]

Attorney John Snee officially filed a petition for writ of habeas corpus, and sought Shirley's release on "the grounds that she is illegally imprisoned." [5]

Rosenberg pulled his evidence together and formally charged Carnahan with three counts of "conduct unbecoming of an officer:

1. On Feb 24 in the ABA Club, and thereafter did intentionally make erroneous and misleading statements in connection with shooting.
2. Did in an unprofessional and inexpert manner handle his revolver so as to permit its discharge.
3. Did associate with a person or persons of questionable repute." [4]

"Bringing," as Rosenberg so eloquently said it, "embarrassment [and] discredit to the Bureau of Police." [4]

The tides began to turn when the Pittsburgh public saw the case for what it was: a corrupt police force attempting to manipulate and abuse a woman who could not defend herself. "Hundreds of persons have stopped me in the streets," Snee reported, "to tell me, 'I hope you get her out.'" Snee further stated that he

80

received multiple random donations of anywhere between $10 and $100 from citizens of Pittsburgh. An anonymous donor was quoted as saying:

> "I am one who hates to see anyone buried because they have had the unfortunate experience to come into contact with the Pittsburgh Police Department." [5]

Pittsburgh Post-Gazette, March 5, 1957.

The Pittsburgh Press

FINAL
Latest Stocks

VOL. 73, No. 256 — TUESDAY, MARCH 6, 1957 — 44 Pages—5 Cents

CARNAHAN FACES TRIAL BOARD

Records 'Lost' In Flatley Pardon Case

Notes Likely 'Destroyed,' Probers Told

Led War on Cigarets
Lung Surgeon Dies of Cancer

Disease Claims Life of Top Foe

17 Britons Killed In Plane Crash

3 Violations Charged

Israeli Mobs Protest Egypt Pullout

Ben-Gurion Faces Tough Fight In Confidence Vote

Third Version Of Shooting Given by Cop

Sun-Telegraph

PITTSBURGH

Cop's Wife Talks In Shooting Probe

Israeli Civilians Marching Home

Record Road Bill Offered By Leader

Democrat, GOP Bloc Back Bill

$40,000 Loan Gone

Quizzed For 15 Minutes

Final Edition

5¢

Favoritism Claimed In Wharf Parking

Dukes Win But Lose NIT Hopes

Civil Defense Jobs Proposed for 4-Fs

Why Do Fathers Desert Families?

Records Offered By Beck's Critic

[1] "Wounded Policeman Gives Third Version of Shooting."
Warren Times Mirror 05 Mar 1957, Tue. P.1, Col. 4.
https://www.newspapers.com/image/56989890

[2] "Lt. Carnahan Changes Story Third Time." *Daily American*, 5
Mar 1957, Tue. P. 2, Col. 7.
https://www.newspapers.com/image/511094459

[3] "Cops Wife Talks in Shooting Probe: Quizzed for 45 Minutes."
Pittsburgh Sun-Telegraph
5 Mar 1957, Tue. Page 3, Col. 5.
https://www.newspapers.com/image/524003258

[4] "Carnahan Faces Trial Board: 3 Violations Charged." *The
Pittsburgh Press,* 5 Mar 1957, Tue. P. 4, Col. 1.
https://www.newspapers.com/image/148057906

[5] "'Free Shirley' Case Mapped by Attorney: Two Moves
Planned to Release Woman in Carnahan Affair." *The Pittsburgh
Press,* 5 Mar 1957, Tue. P. 4, Col. 4.
https://www.newspapers.com/image/148057906

Wednesday, March 6th, 1957
Shirley in County Jail: Day Five

After reviewing all of the evidence, Assistant District Attorney William Claney Smith publicly stated:

"It is now the position of the district attorney's office that Miss Cavanaugh should be freed on bond pending inquiry into events which jailed her." [1]

Regardless, Judge Harry M. Montgomery maintained his decision: Shirley remained held in county jail until she was transferred to the State Industrial Home for Women at Muncy. Montgomery rationalized his reasoning by saying that he "revoked her probation because of Shirley's general course of conduct."[32] [2]

He set a hearing for 1:30 p.m. the next day to "determine whether Shirley actually committed the burglary to which she pleaded guilty." [3]

Snee began to see little hope for a change in Judge Montgomery's convictions and began the next phase of his "Free Shirley" campaign: find another judge. Snee decided to go around the authority of Montgomery and seek out someone with reason. In this case, that someone was Judge Clarence B. Nixon. [2]

Carnahan was discharged from Allegheny General Hospital.

He remained suspended from the police force.

The bullet was still in his thigh. [1]

---

[32] Fuck the patriarchy.

Badly Bent! —By Hungerford

Pittsburgh Post-Gazette, March 6, 1957.

[1] "Attorney Will Seek Freedom for Shirley: Shooting Figure in Jail on Probation Violation: Legality of Plea Questioned." *Pittsburgh Post-Gazette*, 6 Mar 1957, Wed. P. 6, Col. 1. https://www.newspapers.com/image/89450667

[2] "Shirley Asks Liberty: Freedom Near for Shirley? DA Backing Release Bid." *Pittsburgh Sun-Telegraph,* 6 Mar 1957, Wed. P. 1, Col. 1. https://www.newspapers.com/image/524003282

[3] "Shirley Seeks Release From Burglary Term." *Pittsburgh Post-Gazette*, 7 Mar 1957, Thu. P. 1, Col. 6. https://www.newspapers.com/image/89450692

Thursday, March 7th, 1957
Shirley in County Jail: Day Six

As Rosenberg ended his 5 ½ day probe, the *Pittsburgh Post-Gazette* reported:

> "The first concrete evidence that the Police Department deliberately tried to cover up the shooting came to light yesterday on the fifth day of Director Roseberg's investigation."

Pittsburgh Post-Gazette, March 7, 1957

Police Superintendent Francis J. Schafer accused Lieutenant Francis Walsh of failing to properly follow any regulations and rules regarding a shooting, and stated to the press:

> "I would have called for an ambulance and sent the victim to the hospital. I believe I would have put somebody at the door and then started questioning everybody in the place." [1] [2]

The *Pittsburgh Press* published this photo[33] of Shirley, after her burglary trial, being escorted through a courthouse crowd accompanied by the headlines "Shirley Denied Freedom." [3]

[Pittsburgh Post Gazette Archives]

---

[33] When I reached out to the *Post-Gazette* to purchase some of these photos, I was put in touch with Linda Parker, an archivist who only works on Saturdays. Our exchanges were incredibly straightforward and I am deeply grateful for the amount of photos she was able to uncover from the archives for me. When I started collecting newspapers, some of the photos were awfully distorted images of Shirley, so I would purchase them, digitize them and spend as much time as I needed removing cracks and damages and colorizing them. Shirley deserved to look human.

The Pittsburgh Press

VOL. 73, No. 255   THURSDAY, MARCH 7, 1957   WEATHER—Light snow

FINAL
Latest Stocks

56 Pages—5 Cents

COUNTY ENDS FREE FOOD JUNE 1

Face-Lifting For City Hits Snag

Two Slum Cleanup Projects Lost On U. S. Priority List

From Press Washington Bureau

WASHINGTON, March 7—Pittsburgh's future redevelopment schemes have hit a snag.

There's not enough money in the Federal pot.

As a result, the proposed East Liberty and Manchester projects are way down on the list of the Housing and Home Finance Agency.

The agency which is giving two-thirds of the tab for the $6-million-dollar East Liberty slum clearance is waiting for Congress to give it more money.

Panic for Loan

If anyone has requested $75-million of the $90-million dollar authorization for the slum clearance should file an application for a share now.

With over 25 cities asking for it at once, the agency has to come up a process for distributing future cities' requests.

There are three categories and the East Liberty and Manchester projects rate in the third and lowest.

This means a gap in the third and lowest.

Shirley Denied Freedom

CURIOSITY SEEKERS JAM SHIRLEY'S HEARING—Crowds packed the corridors leading to Judge Harry M. Montgomery's courtroom as Shirley Cavanaugh was returned today for a hearing. Police U.S. After Cavanaugh And Vet In the

Police Shakeup Brewing as Result of Probe

Shirley Cavanaugh, the woman in the "Cavanaugh affair," was sent back to jail today by Judge Harry M. Montgomery who refused her freedom on a writ of habeas corpus.

The judge said he will consider allowing Shirley to withdraw a 1954 guilty plea to a charge of burglary and stand trial before a jury.

That could get her liberty on bail.

Other talk across the way in City Hall hinted at a major shakeup in the operation of the Police Bureau.

Cop Shakeup Brewing

Sweeping changes in operations of the Bureau of Police were brewing today as the result of the "Cavanaugh affair," involving...

Shirley Faints In Courtroom

Hundreds of persons crowded the courtroom of Judge Harry M. Montgomery today to get a look at 26-year-old Shirley Cavanaugh the 26-year-old...

Distribution Job Handed To State

$100,000-a-Year Saving Expected By Commissioners

Allegheny County notified the State today that it is getting out of the free food business on June 1.

The fate of nearly 215,000 persons on the surplus food rolls — one out of every seven County residents — will then rest in the hands of the State.

The Commissioners voted the surplus emergency relief program back in the laps of State officials who they think it belongs as they adopted an "austerity" budget for 1957.

It will mean a saving of almost during the first six months of this year but if the program goes over a year it will cost almost...

By Budget Bureau

The Commissioners' action came after they were forced to borrow when it came to agree over how every tax dollar was spending the budget which balances...

Get Braced For Snow Tonight

U.N. Occupies Gaza As Israelis Pull Out

New Occupied Port Mideast Peace As Arabs Jerusalem on Use of Aqaba

Hatchet Death Suspect Sought

Stranger Wanted In Zelienople Case

[1] "Carnahan Coverup is Charged: Asst. Supt. Puts Walsh On the Spot." *Pittsburgh Post-Gazette*, 7 Mar 1957, Thu. P. 1.
https://www.newspapers.com/image/89450692

[2] "5 ½ Day Probe Ends: Draft Report on Police Shooting." The *Indiana Gazette,* Fri. 8 Mar. 1957, P. 1, Col. 2.
https://www.newspapers.com/image/540597581

[3] "Shirley Denied Freedom." *The Pittsburgh Press*, 7 Mar 1957, Thu, P. 1, Col. 2.
https://www.newspapers.com/image/148062693

Friday, March 8th, 1957
Shirley in County Jail: Day Seven

Shirley remained detained in County Jail, and Judge Montgomery indicated that he would make a decision on her ruling next week, "probably Monday afternoon." [1] [3] But Montgomery "is in an unusual situation," The *Post-Gazette* reported, "in which DA Edward C. Boyle joined Defense Attorney John V. Snee in asking that Shirley's guilty plea to [burglary] be thrown out and a jury trial held." [2]

"After considerable investigation," Assistant DA William Claney Smith publicly stated, "we in the district attorney's office question the quality of the Commonwealth's evidence so far as any intent of burglary was concerned." [3]

Both Snee and Smith agreed that actions taken by Judge Montgomery "deprived Shirley of her constitutional rights." Stated Snee, "Shirley is the victim of a tragic miscarriage of justice." [3]

Following through the steps of his "Free Shirley" campaign, Snee officially began his examination of attorney Charles B. Jarrett, Shirley's counsel for her 1954 burglary charge, who was appointed *by the court* of Judge Montgomery. The interview[34] between Snee and Jarrett was telling:

> **Jarrett**: She pleaded guilty before I became involved in the case.
> **Snee**: Do you recall who asked you to represent Shirley?
> **Jarrett**: Judge Montgomery from the bench.
> **Snee**: At what stage in the proceedings?
> **Jarrett**: To the best of my recollection Mrs. Lauterbach had already signed a plea of guilty on an indictment charging burglary.
> **Snee**: There had been no testimony taken?

---

[34] Published in the *Post-Gazette*. [2]

Jarrett: No. I was not in court April 26th, 1954 when Shirley was placed on probation for three years. I had not been advised to be there.

Snee: What did you think the disposition of the burglary case would be?

Jarrett: I was under the impression, from some remark made by Judge Montgomery, that he would be lenient. "Was it because I said she didn't look like a burglar to me?" Montgomery asked, I said it was.

Unbeknownst to many, sitting in the courtroom that day was attorney Marjorie Hanson Matson, a representative from the American Civil Liberties Union (ACLU) who, after hearing the details of the case, stated, "The union would be receptive to a request for help, if necessary." [3]

Courtroom Jammed

Hundreds of curious spectators jammed the courtroom yesterday for a look at the 98-pound defendant.

They included many women, some in mink, and men in Prince Albert coats, and sports jackets.

Those in the back of the courtroom climbed to benches, and others craned over shoulders from the doorways.

SHIRLEY CAVANAUGH AND ATTORNEY SNEE
. . . "I took a picture of my daughter"

Curious crowd attends hearing for Shirley Cavanaugh.

Pittsburgh Press
Friday March 8, 1957

Pittsburgh Sun Telegraph
Friday March 8 1957

[1] "5 ½ Day Probe Ends: Draft Report on Police Shooting." *Indiana Gazette* Fri. 8 Mar. 1957, P. 1, Col. 2. https://www.newspapers.com/image/540597581

[2] "Judge Studies Shirley's Bid For Freedom," *Pittsburgh Post-Gazette*, 8 Mar. 1957, P. 1, Col. 2 & P. 6 Col 2. https://www.newspapers.com/image/89450728

[3] "Shirley Waiting for Her Release: 'Bad Police Must Pay'." *Pittsburgh Sun-Telegraph*, 8 Mar 1957, Fri, P. 3, Col. 1. https://www.newspapers.com/image/524003358

Saturday, March 9th, 1957
Shirley in County Jail: Day Eight

Shirley spent one week in the county jail and the headlines read "Divorcee to Face Shooting Charges," "Prosecution of Shirley is Pressed," and "Shirley Will be Prosecuted Says Officer."

The official report revealed that Superintendent James Slusser intended to charge Shirley with "felonious shooting and assault with intent to kill in connection with the wounding of Acting Lt. Allen Carnahan." Furthermore, Slusser stated Carnahan "will face action before a police trial board if he refuses to appear as a witness." [1]

Divorcee to Face Shooting Charges

PITTSBURGH (AP)—Shirley Cavanaugh, 28-year-old divorcee, will be prosecuted in the shooting of Acting Police Lt. Allen Carnahan, regardless of whether the officer presses charges, says Police Supt. James Slusser.

Miss Cavanaugh is charged with felonious shooting and assault with intent to kill in connection with the wounding of Carnahan in a downtown club Feb. 24. She now is in jail for a probation violation.

Slusser said yesterday that Carnahan, who changed his version of the shooting three times, will face action of the police trial board if he refuses to appear as a witness.

Carnahan, suspended since the shooting, first said it was accidental, then that Miss Cavanaugh did it and finally that it occured in a scuffle with the girl. He has said he will not prosecute her.

Record Argus Sat Mar 9, 1957

[1] "Shirley Will Be Prosecuted Says Officer." *Daily American*, 9 Mar. 1957, Sat. P. 6, Col. 7.
https://www.newspapers.com/image/511094571

Sunday, March 10th, 1957
Shirley in County Jail: Day Nine

Snee reported to the *Sun-Telegraph* that the Pittsburgh public began to support Shirley over Carnahan and the Pittsburgh Police. Snee continued to receive financial donations for Shirley's defense fund. One included a letter telling Shirley to "blast the police department," with a $100 check from the Committee of 70.[35]

Several letters that he received were published in the story "Shirley Finds She's Not Alone." [1]

One letter to Shirley was from a Bethel woman, who wrote:

> "We're relaxed, easy going and shock proof. I certainly would like to see her relaxed to the point where she can eat some good food and gain a little. I repeat, she is more than welcome to make her home with us until she can organize her own life again." [1]

Another letter from a woman in Sarver, Butler County, read:

> "I have been following the story and have become quite interested. If possible I would like to help. Financial help is out, but we do have a comfortable home. I feel every human being is entitled to a fair chance and I think she has been given some bad times." [1]

Louis Glasso, Carnahan's attorney, told *The Pittsburgh Press*:

> "I feel Shirley is being unjustly detained. Both she and Lieutenant Carnahan said the shooting was an accident and that no crime was committed." [2]

---

[35] "A group of objective citizens concerned only that there be honesty and justice in the government of Pittsburgh." [1]

It seemed as if everything was going Shirley's way until …

The *Sun-Telegraph* and the *Daily American* reported that Police Superintendent Slusser and Assistant Superintendent Maloney both, with a sturdy dedication to the law, decided to press charges against Shirley even though Carnahan didn't.

Slusser and Maloney attempted to charge Shirley with "felonious assault and battery and assault with intent to kill."[36] [3] [4]

---

[36] Attorney Brandon Keller explained that they would have needed the backing of the DA, which they didn't have. So it never came to fruition.

[1] "Shirley Finds She's Not Alone." *Pittsburgh Sun-Telegraph,* 10 Mar. 1957, Sun. P. 2, Col. 5.
https://www.newspapers.com/image/524003406

[2] "Carnahan Wants Shirley Freed: Officer Insists Shooting Accident." *The Pittsburgh Press*, 10 Mar. 1957, Sun. Page 2, Col. 8. https://www.newspapers.com/image/148067132

[3] "Shirley Waiting for Her Release: 'Bad Police Must Pay'." *Pittsburgh Sun-Telegraph*, 08 Mar 1957, Fri · P. 3, Col. 1.
https://www.newspapers.com/image/524003358

[4] "Shirley Will Be Prosecuted Says Officer." *Daily American*, 9 Mar. 1957, Sat. P. 6, Col. 7.
https://www.newspapers.com/image/511094571

Monday, March 11th, 1957[37]
Shirley in County Jail: Day Ten

While attorney Louis Glasso reported that Carnahan would stand against both Maloney and Slusser to intercede on behalf of Shirley,[38] Judge Montgomery explained to the *Pittsburgh Post-Gazette* that it didn't matter to him either way:

> "Her sentence (to Muncy) was not for anything she may have done at the Sixth Street club on February 24. That incident merely directed the court's attention to the flagrancy of her probation violations. This investigation disclosed that she had been violating practically every rule of probation ... She continued with her activity of an immoral nature, developing the reputation of being a girl available on call for immoral purposes. She indulged in the use of intoxicants. She left the jurisdiction of the court without permission in the company of male companions, visiting various out-of-state cities including Washington D.C., Wheeling, W. Va., Bellaire, O., and New York City. She associated with known prostitutes. She associated and lived with a person presently charged with prostitution. She should not and will not again have her infractions overlooked and secure her release into society without accounting for them. The only alternatives this court has, are sending her to the Workhouse or County Jail, in neither of which is there any extensive program for women." [3]

---

[37] Republican County Chairman Edward L. Flaherty called The Carnahan Affair an example of "Democratic party sin" and joined the Allegheny County League of Women Voters in urging a federal investigation of the Pittsburgh Police Bureau. [1]

[38] Insisting again that the shooting was accidental. [2]

Pittsburgh Post-Gazette, March 11, 1957

[1] "Police Department Here U.S. Asked to Investigate." *Pittsburgh Post-Gazette* 11 Mar. 1957, Mon. P. 4, Col. 3. https://www.newspapers.com/image/89450789

[2] "Carnahan Will Testify for Shirley in Shooting." *Pittsburgh Post-Gazette,* 11 Mar. 1957, Mon. P. 5, Col. 1. https://www.newspapers.com/image/89450790

[3] "Shirley Loses Her Appeal for Release From Jail." *Pittsburgh Post-Gazette,* 12 Mar. 1957, Tue. P. 9, Col. 3. https://www.newspapers.com/image/89450830

Tuesday, March 12th, 1957
Shirley in County Jail: Day 11

"What is that man trying to do to me? This is my life! If I have to go to Muncy, I won't be a human being anymore. I've seen girls after they've been there. *They're not human!*" [1]

[1] Ferguson, Marilyn "Shirley Cries Like Child at News It's Still Jail." *Pittsburgh Sun-Telegraph,* 12 Mar. 1957, Tue. P. 3, Col. 1. https://www.newspapers.com/image/524003539

Wednesday, March 13th, 1957
Shirley in County Jail: Day 12

Even though Shirley had the support of the entire city of Pittsburgh, attorneys Snee and Glasso, as well as the support of Pittsburgh's District Attorney *and* the ACLU offering to send a lawyer, Judge Montgomery held steady his decision. Shirley was not permitted to enter a new plea for her 1954 burglary charge and she was to be detained — indefinitely. [1]

Snee, recognizing the continuing injustice, went over the head of Judge Montgomery again. This time he sought the aid of Judge Blair Gunther who, upon reviewing the case, immediately instructed the "prothonotary[39] of Superior Court to notify Judge Harry M. Montgomery he *must not* send Shirley Cavanaugh to the State Industrial Home at Muncy until he can rule on her petition to be freed on bail." [2]

'Persecution'

I think it is a shame the way Shirley Cavanaugh is being persecuted. It is just like Russia. It seems the police are just for one another and the poor girl doesn't have a chance. And that judge! How can he hold a person in jail after what he has heard?

Shirley may not have done the right things in the past, but there is not one person who hasn't had something to hide. If that girl is sent to Muncy she will be far worse when she comes out.

CHARLES F. BERNARD
Canonsburg, Pa.

Pgh Sun-Telegraph Wed March 13, 1957

---

[39] A chief clerk of any of various courts of law. [3]

[1] "DA Backs Shirley on Freedom." *Pittsburgh Sun-Telegraph*, 13 Mar. 1957, Wed. P. 2, Col. 8.
https://www.newspapers.com/image/524003570

[2] "Free Shirley, Snee Asks High Court." *The Pittsburgh Press,* 13 Mar. 1957, Wed. P. 1, Col. 1.
https://www.newspapers.com/image/148075015

[3] "Prothonotary" definition.
https://www.merriam-webster.com/dictionary/prothonotary

Thursday, March 14th, 1957
Shirley in County Jail: Day 13

Judge Blair Gunther considered all the evidence and concluded the "right thing to do" was to overrule Judge Montgomery and release Shirley from county jail, setting her bail at $2,000.[40] [1]

When word reached the general public that Shirley "might be released, a large crowd gathered on Ross Street, across from the jail entrance, to get a look at her." [1]

[Pittsburgh Post Gazette Archives]

---

[40] Frank "The Thin Man" Haney was a "ghost" professional bondsman whose slogan was *"Don't Let It Drive You Zany! Call Frank Haney!"* and while Shirley's bail was set at $2,000, Haney, for whatever reason, paid an amount of $5,000 as a "surety bond, free of charge." [1] [2]

Shirley Cheered As She Leaves Jail

Crowd on Hand for Her Release on Bail; Freedom's 'Wonderful,' Woman Says

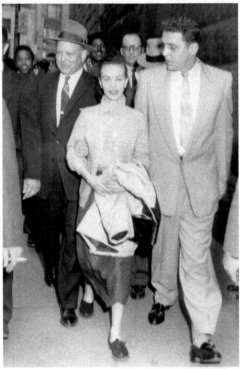

[Pittsburgh Post Gazette Archives]

[Wiki Commons Image]

Among the deputies escorting her was Fran Rogel, bruising Pittsburgh Steelers fullback.

Pgh Press Thurs Mar 14, 1957

[1] "Shirley Cheered As She Leaves Jail: Crowd on Hand for Her Release on Bail; Freedom's Wonderful, Woman Says." *The Pittsburgh Press*, 14 Mar. 1957, Thu. P. 1, Col. 2.
https://www.newspapers.com/image/148076769

[2] "Bail Stickup Gang Captured in 'Rocks'." *The Pittsburgh Press*, 4 Mar. 1960, Fri. P. 1, Col. 4.
https://www.newspapers.com/image/141369548

Friday, March 15th, 1957

Shirley was freed from county jail. Her destination was kept a secret as Snee whisked her away from the gathering crowd of "hundreds [of] spectators [that] gathered in front of the County Jail when she was released." [1]

"My heart is pounding just a bit hard," Shirley stated, "but now that I am free I want to forget everything and just rest." When asked about her thoughts on the crowds that had gathered to support her, she replied:

> "It looks like a lot of people are in my corner. I always said that things would right themselves and now I know I was right. I am very happy over what my attorney has done for me and feel that after a rest everything will turn out all right." [1]

She added:

> "I hope my mother's as happy as I am. I just hope everything will be straightened out so I can lead a whole life again. It will be good." [2]

The *Post-Gazette* reported:

> "The release of Shirley on bond yesterday is not the end of the troubles brought about by Judge Harry Montgomery [...] Judge Blair Gunther also ruled that Snee's contention she was illegally found guilty of the burglary charge will be reviewed by the Superior Court when it sits here Monday, April 8th." [1]

In releasing Shirley on bond, Judge Gunther was quoted as saying:

> "I am just doing what I believe is right. Everyone of us, regardless of our position, is entitled to the full protection of our rights. We are presumed innocent until proof of guilt is presented in accordance with the rules of the law. The same principle, especially today, must apply to us all. It is only fair and right to refrain from passing judgment on any man or woman until all the facts are in." [1]

[1] "Her Court Troubles far From Over: Carnahan Shooting Case Figure Rushed to Hide-away by Lawyer; Bail Ends Two-Week Legal Battle." *Pittsburgh Post-Gazette,* 15 Mar. 1957, Fri. P. 1, Col. 3. https://www.newspapers.com/image/89450926

[2] "Wasn't Easy to Get Out: Shirley Trying to Forget Now." *Pittsburgh Sun-Telegraph,* 15 Mar. 1957, Fri. P. 3, Col. 2. https://www.newspapers.com/image/524001136

Shirley Wins a Round

WE ARE glad that Superior Judge Blair F. Gunther found grounds upon which to free Shirley Cavanaugh from jail pending a hearing for a new trial. Until now, this girl has had less than a fair break at the hands of the law.

Consider, for example, the burglary charge upon which she was sentenced in 1954. It involved the entry of the home of her ex-husband's mother to pick up several small personal possessions. An Assistant District Attorney says now that there was no basis for a burglary charge.

But Shirley got three years on probation when she pleaded guilty, apparently as the result of poor advice. And when she was charged with shooting Police Lieutenant Allen Carnahan in an after-hours drinking club, she was promptly clapped into jail for parole violation.

There is no doubt that Shirley violated the terms of her parole. But neither is there any doubt that she had been violating them for a long time, with the knowledge if not with the connivance and at the pleasure of policemen.

So long as she was useful to them, the police were quite content with her infractions. It was only after she was involved in a shooting that the police took any interest in enforcing the terms of her parole. How, then, can one avoid the feeling that the police have ill-used this girl?

When it became evident that Shirley was in a position to make trouble, she was promptly put into cold storage. That made it look as if her arrest and parole revocation were part of a police cover-up attempt.

So, as we said, we are glad that Judge Gunther has freed her under bond pending further attempts at justice. We certainly don't condone Shirley's notorious misbehavior but, like any other citizen, she is entitled to the protection of her rights.

Pittsburgh Post-Gazette Sat, March 16, 1957

Shirley Spends Day With Niece, Nephew

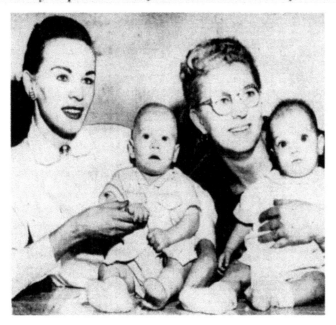

Pgh Post Gazette Mon Mar 18, 1957

Shirley's illegal detention came to an end. An image of her and her mother, niece, and nephew was printed on the front page of the *Pittsburgh Post-Gazette*. An image that spoiled the narrative that Shirley is simply a problem human who is "incapable of deep seated emotional attachments" and whose "maternal instinct is not normal." [1]

When Shirley was freed from the confines of a careless system bent on her manipulation and usefulness, when she was free to just be — a different side was witnessed; family, a bond was shared.

[1] R.H. Kiefer, M. D. "Shirley Cavanaugh (Lauterbach): Analysis." The Behavior Clinic, 636 County Office Building, April 14, 1954

Tuesday, March 19th, 1957

Rosenberg dished out public scoldings to the following:

ROSENBERG RAPS TOP POLICE FOR CARNAHAN CASE BUNGLE

LT. FRANCIS WALSH   CAPT. GEORGE PURVIS   LT. ALLEN CARNAHAN   SUPT. JAMES W. SLUSSER   LAWRENCE J. MALONEY   ADAM GEISLER

The Pittsburgh Press Tue Mar 19 1957

➢ Police Superintendent James. W. Slusser, who "knew Carnahan could not have shot himself, yet 'seemed to be vague' on what action he was taking to find out who did it." Criticizing him further for his "mental and physical sluggishness."

➢ Assistant Superintendent Lawrence J. Maloney, who "accepted the word of a fellow officer and yet made no attempt to procure evidence which would sustain the word of a man in whom he believed."

➢ Assistant Superintendent Adam Geisler, who "whisked Miss Cavanaugh's secret diary and personal photographs out of her apartment without a search warrant." Rosenberg criticized him further for "failure to check Carnahan's clothes for a bullet hole."

➢ Captain George Purvis, who "failed to check Carnahan's clothing and who allowed a material witness (Marie Linden, Miss Cavanaugh's roommate) to leave the state during the investigation."

➢ Lieutenant Francis Walsh, who "failed to use his knowledge or training," was suspended for 10 days, reprimanded and ordered transferred to River Patrol for "leaving the club with the wounded detective while witnesses were milling about

117

inside and failing to notify the radio control center that a man had been shot."

Rosenberg's punishments, reprimands, and shuffling of the police officers involved ultimately resulted in the full disbandment of the Pittsburgh Vice and Narcotic Squad.

As for Carnahan, Rosenberg intended to "personally prosecute him when he is physically able to face a trial board." [1] [2] [3]

[1] "Probe Officer Suspended in Club Shooting, Walsh Suspended for Handling of Carnahan Case." *The Pittsburgh Press,* 19 Mar .1957, Tue. P. 1, Col. 8. https://www.newspapers.com/image/148008296

[2] "Slusser, 3 Aides handed Carnahan Case Reprimand." *Pittsburgh Post-Gazette,* 20 Mar. 1957, Wed. P. 1 https://www.newspapers.com/image/89451052

[3] "Carnahan Trial Pushed by Director." *Pittsburgh Sun-Telegraph,* 20 Mar. 1957, Wed. P. 3, Col. 1. https://www.newspapers.com/image/524001500

[4] "Rosenberg Raps top Police for Carnahan Case Bungle, Officers Gagged on Report." *The Pittsburgh Press*, 19 Mar .1957, Tue. P. 1. https://www.newspapers.com/image/148008296

Pittsburgh Post-Gazette, March 20, 1957.

---

[41] Amazing.

The Law, Spelled Out

FOR entering her former mother-in-law's house to get back articles she said belonged to her, Shirley Cavanaugh, the call-girl in the Carnahan case, was charged with burglary several years ago and put on probation when she pleaded guilty.

And when police under Assistant Superintendent Adam Geisler were seeking a clue to the Cavanaugh girl's whereabouts, after Lt. Allen Carnahan was shot Feb. 24, they got into her apartment and confiscated a box of papers and letters.

★ ★ ★

The police had no search warrant to enter Shirley's apartment, although the Constitution explicitly states that "the right of the people to be secure in their persons, houses, papers and effects, against unreasonable searches and seizures, shall not be violated."

What was the difference between Shirley's action and the police action?

What standing in law did the police action have? Fortunately, Director of Public Safety Louis Rosenberg devoted part of his report on the Carnahan case to spelling out the rights of citizens.

He said:

"The fundamental law protects all persons against undue and illegal search and seizure. The law provides a method by which search and seizure must be done. When Assistant Superintendent Geisler had occasion, or reason, to search the apartment of Shirley Cavanaugh for the purpose of ascertaining her whereabouts, there was ample time for him to procure a search warrant.

"This is but a matter of minutes, and as the Assistant Superintendent knows, may be procured at any time from any alderman or magistrate. If there had been an emergency and the few minutes necessary for procuring the search warrant would have menaced public safety, then he might have proceeded without a search warrant, but there was no such emergency here and the omission of the Assistant Superintendent to procure a search warrant was a flagrant violation of law and his duties."

★ ★ ★

It should not have been necessary for the Safety Director to spell out the meaning of the search and seizure clause in the U. S. Constitution. But in view of what happened in the Carnahan case, it's a good thing he did.

The U. S. Supreme Court ruled long ago that this protection applies to all, whether accused of crime or not, and that it is the duty of all entrusted with enforcement of the laws to give it force and effect.

The Pittsburgh Press Fri Mar 22, 1957

Saturday, March 23rd, 1957

At this point in time, one goal became the sole focus: have Shirley's 1954 Burglary conviction *nolle prossed*.

And who better to help Shirley out of these charges than the American Civil Liberties Union who, on Friday, March 22nd, 1957, revealed "plans for possible intervention in Shirley's guilty pleas to her 1954 burglary charge."

According to the *Pittsburgh Post-Gazette*:

> "Attorney Sylvan Libson, co-chairman of the union's legal committee, said a legal assistant, Lloyd Fuge, has been instructed to check the court records of the 1954 conviction and the testimony at the habeas corpus hearing recently before Judge Harry M. Montgomery.
>
> Fuge will also check the accounts of newspaper stories as well as those of unofficial observers to determine if Shirley's constitutional rights have been denied.
>
> If this be the case, Lisbon said, then the American Civil Liberties Union will petition the right to intervene on behalf of the girl as a friend of the court." [1]

This was a great turning point for Shirley's case, as it seemed here, with the potential involvement of the ACLU on the horizon, all eyes turned to Carnahan — who was demanded to quit the police force by, apparently, the *entire* city of Pittsburgh.

Mayor David Lawrence concluded his tour of West Germany and immediately began to "rip police for sloppy work" further warning, "It had better not happen again." [2] He stated further that he would "stand on the Rosenberg report [as] the director is meticulously honest and will do the right thing."

123

CARNAHAN SUSPENDED FOR YEAR

Marilyn's Husband Guilty of Contempt

Red Quiz Fight Lost By Miller

Refusal to Answer Questions Ruled Unlawful by Judge

25 Persons Indicted In Pike Probe

New Link Seen No Relation To January Burn

Britain Fires 2nd H-Bomb In Pacific

As Carnahan Draws a Year's Suspension

Ex-Constable Goes to Pen

Warm, Rain Likely Today

Shirley Refuses To Testify In Shooting of Cop

Police Trial Board Recommends Layoff After Finding Former Boss Of Vice Squad Guilty on 3 Counts

Beck Gives Widow Share Of Profits

The Pittsburgh Press

FINAL
Latest Stocks

VOL. 73, No. 280

MONDAY, APRIL 1, 1957

60 Pages—5 Cents

POLICE WORK 'SLOPPY'--MAYOR

Lawler Pleased

Sponsors Balk At Road Blast

Constructors Refuse to Approve Resolution Ripping Department

New Roads to Set Record in State

Federal Program Funds Assured

Subscribers Offered New Contract

Higher Premium Buys 30-70 Days Hospital Care

Blue Cross Plan Expanded

Drama at 40,000 Feet Over North Hills

Pilot Acts Fast in Jet Collision

Airman Shoots Self From Plane

Lawrence Arrives In New York

Rips Handling Of Carnahan Shooting Case

'Surprise Witness' At Cops' Trial Board

Six Killed In B-25 Crash

Shirley May Get Support

The American Civil Liberties Union yesterday revealed plans for possible intervention in the case of Shirley Cavanaugh's guilty plea to a 1954 burglary charge.

Attorney Sylvan Libson, co-chairman of the union's legal committee, said a legal assistant, Lloyd Fuge, has been instructed to check the court records of the 1954 conviction and the testimony at the habeas corpus hearing recently before Judge Harry M. Montgomery.

(Shirley pleaded guilty, in 1954, to "burglarizing" the home of in-laws, but claimed she only removed personal belongings.)

Fuge will also check the accounts of newspaper stories as well as those of unofficial observers to determine if Shirley's constitutional rights have been denied.

If this be the case, Libson said, then the American Civil Liberties Union will petition the right to intervene, on behalf of the girl, as a friend of the court.

**Pgh Post Gazette
Sat Mar 23, 1957**

125

[1] "Shirley May Get Support." *Pittsburgh Post-Gazette*, 23 Mar. 1957, Sat. P. 5, Col. 2.
https://www.newspapers.com/image/89451162

[2] "Lawrence Arrives in New York, Mayor Rips Police for Sloppy Work." *The Pittsburgh Press,* 1 Apr. 1957, Mon. P. 1.
https://www.newspapers.com/image/147892271

Shirley Case Cools Wives On Cop Jobs

By J. JAMES MOORE

Pittsburgh women don't want their husbands to become city policemen.

The apparent reason is the recent police shooting involving Police Lt. Allen Carnahan in a Downtown after-hour club.

Shirley Cavanaugh has been charged with the shooting.

The fact that the city's housewives are opposed to their husbands becoming city policemen has shown up plainly in the files of the Civil Service Commission.

●

ONLY 800 MEN FILED for the patrolman examination which will be given in Schenley High School on May 25.

Secretary and chief examiner of the commissioner James F. McShane said he originally expected 1,600 men to take the test — twice as many as filed.

But that was before Carnahan was shot in the ABA Club, 136 Sixth Ave., on Feb. 24.

Two years ago more than 1,100 men took the patrolman exam.

Persons connected with the Civil Service Commission and the Police Bureau blame the low number of applicants on publicity that followed the shooting.

●

SEVERAL MEN while filing their papers for this year's examination even said:

"I'm doing this against my wife's wishes."

One man said:

"I'll get shot too if my wife finds out that I'm after a police job."

Carnahan was the former head of the city's narcotics and vice squad. He has been suspended pending a hearing before the Police Trial Board.

●

THE HEARING has never been held despite the fact Carnahan was seen in front of City Hall last Wednesday.

Reports around City Hall are that the hearing has been delayed until after the primary election on Tuesday May 21.

Safety Director Louis Rosenberg said he is ready to hold the hearing just as soon as Carnahan is ready.

Pgh Sun Telgraph Sun May 5, 1957

Tuesday, May 7th, 1957

Carnahan went before a police trial board for his interrogation. He testified under oath that the shooting was entirely accidental and he wished for no charges to be brought against Shirley.

Accordingly, Shirley was freed from any wrongdoing regarding the shooting of Carnahan. [1] [2]

After 72 days, the bullet was removed from Carnahan's leg and sent to the crime laboratory. [3]

The Pittsburgh Press

FINAL
— Baseball —
Latest Stocks

VOL. 73, No. 337 · TUESDAY, MAY 28, 1957 · 40 Pages—5 Cents

SHIRLEY FREE IN COP SHOOTING

Murder, Suicide Hinted By Police

New Wilmington Double Death Investigated

Bitter State Debate
GOP Sits Tight On Budget Cut
Determined to Keep Slashes Despite Volley of Protests

East Liberty Store Robbed Third Time
Official Plea: At Flooring Republic, Ready for Return

Berserk Killer Holds Off Capture

'Accidental,' Lt. Carnahan Tells Court
Woman Silent At 5-Minute Police Hearing

U. S. Sets Off Nevada A-Blast

Ike Joins Bonn Chief In German Unity Plea

Pittsburgh Post-Gazette
One of America's Great Newspapers

Final City Edition
FOR WANT ADS — CALL
EXpress 1-4789

VOL. 30—NO. 238 · In Three Sections · WEDNESDAY MORNING, MAY 29, 1957 · Telephone Atlantic 1-6700

Dodger, Giant Shifts To West Coast OKd

Next Move Up to Clubs, Giles Says

Shirley Is Freed In Cop Shooting
Carnahan Testifies Under Oath He Was Wounded Accidentally

Industry Asked For Budget Aid

Syrians Bring Confusion to Hospital

Murder And Suicide Suspected
New Wilmington Girl, 19, Strangled; Man, 29, Shot Dead

Berserk Sailor Kills Ensign, Shoots Another

U. S. Sets Off First Atomic Blast of 1957

[1] "Shirley Won't Testify at Cop Hearing: However, Carnahan Will Say Shooting Was Accidental." *Pittsburgh Post-Gazette* 28 May 1957, Tue. P. 21, Col. 2.
https://www.newspapers.com/image/87920896

[2] "Shirley Cavanaugh to Decline to Testify at Shooting Hearing." *Daily Republican*, 28 May 1957, Tue. P. 5, Col. 8.
https://www.newspapers.com/image/59167221

[3] "Carnahan Bullet Report Awaited." *The Pittsburgh Press*, 07 May 1957, Tue. P. 11, Col. 3.
https://www.newspapers.com/image/148046175

Saturday June 8, 1957

As The Carnahan Affair reached its conclusion, both Safety Director Rosenberg *and* Mayor David Lawrence stated their desire and intention to have Carnahan removed from the force. As such, Carnahan, disgracefully, put in his resignation as a policeman, stating:

> "With deep regret, I herewith tender my resignation as a patrolman from the Pittsburgh Police Department. It seems that this is the only course left to prevent any further embarrassment from publicity to me, my family and the many fine officers with whom I have worked for the past 15 years." [1]

Rosenberg concluded his involvement with one final statement:

> "I have accepted his resignation, after all, I didn't show any hesitancy at the hearing that we wanted Carnahan off the force. His resignation serves our purpose the same as a dismissal." [1]

Furthermore, Carnahan was no longer eligible for a pension, and while he could have applied for reinstatement in the force, Rosenberg "[had] no doubt that [he] would turn him down." [1]

Regarding her burglary charge, Shirley stated, "Lou (Attorney Louis Glass) said it will cost about $90 to have that *nolle prossed*. Al (Carnahan) is paying him." [2]

Superior Court Judge Chester H. Rhodes granted her permission to enter a plea of innocence in her 1954 burglary trial, which trickled down to Court of Common Pleas Judge Henry Ellenbogen, who also granted her the right to change her plea to not guilty.

A new court date, Monday, Jan. 19th, 1958, was set for Shirley's 1954 burglary charge. [2] [3] [4]

Former Head of Vice-Narcotics Squad Turns in His Badge

Carnahan Quits Police Under Fire

Cop Suspended in Club Shooting Resigns After 15 Years on Force

Acting Lieutenant Allen Carnahan yesterday resigned from the Police Department under fire.

The former head of the vice and narcotics squad apparently beat Mayor David L. Lawrence to the punch and quit before he got fired.

The mayor, it was authoritatively reported at City Hall, had planned to spurn the recommendation of a Police

An editorial, "Carnahan Resigns," Page 10.

Trial Board to suspend Carnahan for a year and was going to dismiss him.

Carnahan's downfall terminated 15 years on the force, during which he won the designation of a "good cop" and commendations from his superiors.

It stemmed from the incident in the early-morning hours of February 24 when Carnahan was shot by his own gun in the ABA Club, Sixth Street. His name was linked with that of Shirley Cavanaugh, 28, who was acquitted of felonious shooting in connection with the affair.

The trial board, after a hearing May 31, recommended Carnahan be suspended for one year for conduct unbecom-

ing an officer. That left the final decision in the hands of Mayor Lawrence.

Yesterday, at about 9:45 a. m., Safety Director Louis Rosenberg took the transcript of the trial board hearing to Mayor Lawrence. He returned to his office and was leaving it again when Carnahan and his attorney, Louis C. Glasso, approached.

Glasso handed Director Rosenberg a letter of resignation, signed by Carnahan, which said:

"With deep regret, I herewith tender my resignation as a patrolman from the Pittsburgh Police Department. It seems that this is the only course left to prevent any further embarrassment from publicity to me, my family and the many fine police officers with whom I have worked for the past 15 years."

Then Carnahan, without

ALLEN CARNAHAN
Turns in Badge No. 202.

saying a word, handed the safety director his badge, No. 202.

Rosenberg left no doubt that he was glad Carnahan is no longer a member of the police force. The city administration had asked the police trial

'Closed Case,' Mayor Says

board to dismiss Carnahan.

"I have accepted his resignation," Director Rosenberg said. "After all, I didn't show any hesitancy at the hearing that we wanted Carnahan off the force. His resignation serves our purpose the same as a dismissal."

"It's a closed case," Mayor Lawrence commented. "But I hope it will be a lesson to other city employes."

Director Rosenberg said Carnahan, who had five years to go to become eligible for a pension, now has no pension status. He said if Carnahan ever applies for reinstatement it would be up to the safety director to accept or reject such a request.

Rosenberg left no doubt that if Carnahan ever would apply for reinstatement he would turn him down.

Carnahan, 46, of 3625 Harbison Street, Northside, was appointed to the police force August 3, 1942. He walked beats and served as a plainclothesman before being transferred to the detective bureau in 1952. Shortly afterwards, Carnahan was named head of the vice and narcotics squad.

Pittsburgh Post-Gazette Thursday, January 8, 1959

42

---

[42] Fantastic.

[1] "Former Head of Vice-Narcotics Squad Turns in His Badge. Carnahan Quits Police Under Fire." *Pittsburgh Post-Gazette*, 8 June 1957, Sat. P. 13, Col. 6.
https://www.newspapers.com/image/89456486

[2] "Shirley Given New Start, Granted Another Chance." *Pittsburgh Sun-Telegraph*, 11 Jun 1957, Tue. P. 1, Col. 1.
https://www.newspapers.com/image/523974848

[3] "Court Wipes Out Shirley's '54 Plea, She Wins Victory on Burglary Court." *The Pittsburgh Press*, 11 June 1957, Tue. P. 1, Col. 7. https://www.newspapers.com/image/148049244

[4] "Shirley Will Get New Trial." *Pittsburgh Sun-Telegraph*, 29 Aug 1957, Thu. P. 3, Col. 3.
https://www.newspapers.com/image/524019968

Pittsburgh Post-Gazette, July 13, 1957.

[43] Good luck, Rosenberg.

Calendar of World and District News for 1957

25—City Detective Allen Carnahan admits woman acquaintance shot him in leg in early hours at Downtown club.

26—Shirley Cavanaugh, woman in Carnahan shooting, gives up to police.

3—Police stage "surrender" of call girl Shirley Cavanaugh in Carnahan shooting case.

5—Acting Police Lieutenant Allen D. Carnahan to face police trial board in shooting incident.

19—Police Superintendent James Slusser, three aides, handed reprimand by Safety Director Rosenberg as result of Carnahan shooting probe.

28—Shirley Cavanaugh cleared of charge of shooting suspended Detective Lieutenant Allen Carnahan.

Pittsburgh Post Gazette Tue Dec 31 1957

"I have love in me the likes of which you can scarcely imagine and rage the likes of which you would not believe. If I cannot satisfy the one, I will indulge the other."

Mary Shelley, from "Frankenstein"

The Teitelbaum Probe

In May of 1958, approximately one year after the conclusion of The Carnahan Affair, U.S. Attorney Hubert I. Teitelbaum began the "first and most thoroughly coordinated crackdown of its kind ever taken by the [Pennsylvania] Government" by establishing a 25-county open file of "every major criminal and underworld figure from Point Marion to Erie PA." [1] [2]

In doing so, Teitelbaum created a task force which teamed together the following agencies: FBI, Narcotics Bureau, Internal Revenue Service, Immigration Service, The Post Office Department, Alcohol Tax Bureau, and the T-Men.[44]

Each agency shared the same five goals:

➢ Identify the top racketeers and underworld figures operating in their specifically assigned county
➢ Identify the principal types of illegal activities they were involved in
➢ Establish whether they were operating alone or if they were associated with top underworld figures either locally or nationally
➢ Supply Federal authorities with any investigative material local police officials may have had on these men that may have been able to be used in Teitelbaum's investigation
➢ Identify any possible violation of Federal laws these men may have committed [2]

Less than six months later, Teitelbaum reported on his findings, stating he "now has reliable evidence that high police officials in Pittsburgh have been accepting bribes from racketeers to protect the numbers and gambling rackets."[45] [3]

---

[44] T-Men, I learned, are agents of the treasury.

[45] And also, as we learned in the case of The Carnahan Affair, brothels.

Angry Shirley Talks and Talks

Lists Names And Places

Police, brass force pointed questions in a recital of Shirley's revelations—Page 5.

By MARILYN FERGUSON

Scorned by the two men who meant most in her life, Shirley Cavanaugh turned last night to one with a burning interest in what she has to say—U. S. Attorney Hubert I. Teitelbaum.

Sun-Tele Exclusive

And Shirley, former call-girl, had plenty to tell—about police and rackets.

She minced no words before Teitelbaum, two assistants, two federal stenographers and a Sun-Telegraph reporter.

She involved one of her ex-loves, former Acting Police Lt. Allen Carnahan; a Pittsburgh policeman and a federal narcotics agent.

SHIRLEY CAVANAUGH
. . . woman scorned

Her latest boyfriend, a racketeer's son, has left her, Shirley said.

Alone, Shirley is a child, but she also is a woman scorned. Before last night's talk, she said:

"You know, this is the first time I've been tough. But nobody's looking out for Shirley anymore."

EIGHTEEN MONTHS AGO in anger at Carnahan, Shirley dictated a statement about Pittsburgh police affairs to Attorney John Y. Teitelbaum. It was Thursday when Knox told the statement were superseded by Teitelbaum. Knox kept the secret under the lawyer-client relationship.

Confronted with it the next day before a federal grand jury, Shirley broke. Last night she broke even further.

Teitelbaum was specifically interested in three lines of questions. Shirley, with "nothing to lose but," lost her fear of threats "made up and down Fifth Ave." was told him the answers.

TEITELBAUM WAS interested in an alleged deal made by a narcotics king, a Pittsburgh police detective and one of the federal men. Shirley told him she was in New York when the payoff was made.

She also told that she was told what a payoff was made to a Pittsburgh police detective.

...by a Hill District prostitute. She never remembered that she was wearing a pink gown and left "dirty" after she witnessed the transaction.

Teitelbaum said Shirley is sure she had difficulty answering many of his questions but she did answer them.

She said:

"I used to be able to walk for free and breathe again. I've been sick but I want to get told over with."

SHIRLEY'S PAST is one many readers cannot tolerate. It is not pretty. Shirley is a woman she smiles. She has a gay, quick sense of humor...

...many cannot understand, but not the laugh, after what she has known and not known.

Shirley admitted to Teitelbaum that so sad that five years was a gift bought by a racketeer's payoff. For half the interview Teitelbaum had the ring. Shirley asked for it and put it back. She said:

"If you want the ring, you'd know where to find it. If you want to shut it to him, I'll go with your-wearing it. But I'd feel lost without it."

SHIRLEY HAD THINGS to say and never in shame in connection with the call girl racket locally and the trouble with law enforcement officers.

She tasted hysteria when she told of her first experience with a call to a doctor's house and a telephone call to the "booties" in a high police official. It halted the procedure.

Finally said:

"She ran to the John Doe warrant in front of them (the raiders) after she hung up, and then left."

WHEN SHE FINISHED talking to the United States Attorney, she remarked:

"I feel a hundred per cent better. Maybe it's bad because I don't care about anything anymore."

Pittsburgh Sun Telegraph Tue Oct 28, 1958

And on October 22nd, 1958, it was reported that Shirley was responsible for many of the leads that guided Teitelbaum towards this evidence ...

"I never made use of it [before] because I thought too much of it was hearsay," attorney John Snee stated as he delivered to Teitelbaum a 22-page "secret revenge file" written by Shirley in March of 1957, while she was being illegally detained in county jail. The file was a tell-all regarding not only her relationship with the Pittsburgh Police Bureau, but also everything she witnessed regarding bribery and corruption within the police force. [4] [5]

Accordingly, Shirley was called as a witness and her 22-page "secret revenge file" was, privately, dictated to the jury. Upon leaving the courtroom Shirley kept herself silent in front of the press. Earning her the, truly awesome, headline, "It's Shirley ... The Sphinx."

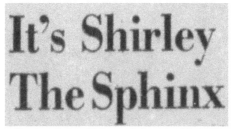

It's Shirley The Sphinx

Pittsburgh Sun Telegraph Sat Oct 25, 1958

And although it had been 16 months since The Carnahan Affair reached its conclusion, Shirley was repeatedly called out as an ex-prostitute, former call-girl, ex-burglar, ex-lover of Carnahan, etc., and the whole Carnahan Affair was paraphrased in every article that mentioned her.

The rehashing of all she wished to leave behind hardened Shirley further. In her penultimate interview with Marilyn Ferguson titled "Angry Shirley Talks and Talks, Lists Names and Places," Shirley stated her parting words with the press:

> "You know, this is the first time I've been tough. But nobody's looking out for Shirley anymore. I feel a hundred percent better ... Maybe it's just because I don't care about anything anymore." [6]

As far as whether or not Shirley's 22-page "revenge file" was able to be put to good use remained opaque. When asked, however, Teitelbaum stated that he was developing more "pointed questions" based on "substantial evidence Shirley gave [to him]." He concluded his statement by saying, "... [regarding] police officials ... This time, they will not be able to say 'I don't know.'" [7]

The Teitelbaum Probe concluded behind closed doors while providing an overwhelming supply of evidence and statements against police and racketeers, as Teitelbaum promised, from Point Marion to Erie, Pennsylvania. Many police were fired, reassigned, suspended, or resigned disgracefully. Many racketeers had individual cases opened against them as well.

And Shirley's time with the Pittsburgh Police, finally, came to an end.

Shirley Quizzed by Jury

Shirley Cavanaugh was an early witness before the Federal Grand Jury checking into charges of bribery.

Friend of Ex-Head Of Vice Squad Goes Before U. S. Probers

Shirley Cavanaugh, former sweetheart of then acting police Lieutenant Allen Carnahan, whose accidental shooting touched off a police scandal in 1957, yesterday testified before a Federal Grand Jury probing into police bribery charges.

Pittsburgh Post Gazette Thu Oct 23 1958

[1] "A Letter From Home: Blue Book." *The Pittsburgh Press,* 10 May 1958, Sat. P. 8, Col. 8.
https://www.newspapers.com/image/149517215

[2] "25-County Probe: U.S. Questions DAs on District Rackets. Teitelbaum Queries 25 County Chiefs to Get Line on Crime Ringleaders." *The Pittsburgh Press,* 25 May 1958, Sun. P. 12, Col. 5. https://www.newspapers.com/image/149518229/

[3] "U.S. To Probe Bribe Case, Cops: Racket Payoffs Still Going On, Official Says." *The Pittsburgh Press,* 16 Sep 1958, Tue. P. 1. https://www.newspapers.com/image/147749723

[4] "Bribe Jury Hears 'Police Secrets: Carnahan Case Girl Certain to Testify at Probe Again.'" *The Pittsburgh Press,* 23 Oct 1958, Thu.P. 10, Col. 3.
https://www.newspapers.com/image/147815329

[5] "Probe Hunts 'Payoffs' in Carnahan Affair, Carnahan Quiz May Engulf Entire Force." *The Pittsburgh Press,* 2 Mar 1957, Sat. P. 1. https://www.newspapers.com/image/148043980/

[6] Ferguson, Marilyn "Angry Shirley Talks and Talks, Lists Names and Places." *Pittsburgh Sun-Telegraph,* 28 Oct 1958, Tue. P. 1, Col. 1.
https://www.newspapers.com/image/524525809

[7] Ferguson, Marilyn. "Shirley Tells of Night She Shot Carnahan.'" *Pittsburgh Sun-Telegraph,* 29 Oct. 1958, P. 3, Col. 1. https://www.newspapers.com/image/524526048

Carnahan is now employed as a "security guard" by a super market chain.

sible link with police officers.

Suspended From Force

Suspended from the force after being wounded in both legs in an after hours club, Carnahan is now employed as a "security guard" by a super market chain.

Carnahan was shot with his own gun during a scuffle with Shirley Cavanaugh, an ex-call girl friend who turned over a 22-page statement about alleged racket payoff to police to the jury last October.

The Cavanaugh statement was made after she was released from jail after being charged with the shooting.

Carnahan had at first claimed he shot himself accidentally and then named Shirley as the person who shot him.

Shortly after the shooting Shirley told newsmen she had a romance with Carnahan and had asked him to divorce his wife.

ALLEN CARNAHAN
Questioned for one hour.

46

Pittsburgh Post-Gazette Thursday, January 8, 1959

---

[46] Excellent.

Shirley won the right to a new trial for her burglary charge. A trial where she could be represented appropriately and by competent counsel. However, the moment Shirley appeared in court something unexpected happened: Judge Clarence B. Nixon dropped the whole thing. No new court case, no burglary charge, no three-year probation.

"All this trouble has now come to an end, and I'm happy and relieved that it's all over," Shirley stated to the press. [1]

Shirley Free in Theft

Ex-Call Girl Thinks Her Attorney Did 'Grand Job'; She's Going South

SHIRLEY CAVANAUGH
State wouldn't prosecute.

Pgh Post Gazette Wed Jan 21, 1959

The burglary charge was *nolle prossed* and as a result of that — Shirley should never have been placed on probation. Therefore on February 24ᵗʰ, 1957, at The ABA, Shirley could not have violated the terms *of* that probation.

Shirley Cavanaugh, attorney John Snee, and Safety Director Louis Rosenberg succeeded.

In a rare example of justice, a 28-year-old sex worker with a record of assault and battery of a police officer, keeping an assignation house, keeping a bawdy house, and prostitution, stood up against the Pittsburgh Police Bureau and won.

The Vice and Narcotic Squad remained entirely disbanded.

Carnahan was no longer a cop and found work as a security guard in a supermarket chain.

Maloney eventually became another disgraced officer and was busted for tax evasion and accepting "bags of cash" as bribes from multiple racketeers. [2]

Eugene Coon, the Sheriff of Allegheny County, spent the last years of his life in the throes of severe alcoholism and anger mismanagement. In 1994, Coon was placed under ankle-monitored house arrest for an "incident" which occurred on November 6th, 1994. While Coon was napping, his neighbors were playing music at their children's birthday party, and Coon didn't like this. He ended up firing several shots from his rifle — into the child's birthday party. [3]

As for Walsh, Slusser, and the rest of them? Unremarkable lives that came to equally unremarkable ends.

As for Rosenberg and Snee, see the acknowledgments section at the end of this book. Each of them deserved their own pages and spotlight.

[1] "Burglary Charge Dropped, Shirley is Free, and in Love, Too." *Pittsburgh Sun-Telegraph,* 20 Jan 1959, Tue. P. 3, Col. 2.
https://www.newspapers.com/image/524018839

[2] Browne, Joseph P. "US Indicts Maloney on Taxes. City Hall Jittery: 'Other Shoe' Awaited in Maloney Case." *Pittsburgh Post-Gazette,* 19 Dec. 1964, Sat. P. 1.
https://www.newspapers.com/image/88152297

[3] "Sheriff Coon Is Placed on House Arrest, 6 Months' Electronic Monitoring for Firing Rifle Toward Neighbors." *Pittsburgh Post-Gazette,* 19 Jan 1996, Fri. P. 17, Col. 1.
https://www.newspapers.com/image/89673875

Sunday, January 25th, 1959

Shirley Cavanaugh disappeared from public awareness in 1959, with one final newspaper article titled "Shirley Wed in Virginia." The article showed a brilliant, genuinely smiling Shirley and was an announcement of her marriage to a man named John Garretson.

Shirley Wed In Virginia

Shirley Cavanaugh is married again.

The former call girl and John H. Garretson, 26, of East McKeesport, were married in a civil ceremony at Winchester, Va., on Dec. 27.

Records show that they were married by Robert M. Grim, the equivalent of a justice of the peace.

Just last week, Shirley, 30, said she hoped to get married "eventually" after she appeared at a court hearing which cleared her of a long-standing burglary charge.

Shirley gained a large chunk of newspaper space when former policeman Allen Carnahan was wounded by his own gun in a Downtown after-hours club.

Shirley was with him and Carnahan blamed her. She blamed him.

Last October she appeared before a federal grand jury probing alleged payoffs to police brass.

SHIRLEY CAVANAUGH
. . . married again
Sun-Telegraph Photo

Pittsburgh Sun Telegraph Sun Jan 25, 1959

"I bid you farewell, I don't know when I'll be back.
They're moving us tomorrow to that tower down the track
But you'll be hearing from me baby, long after I'm gone."

Leonard Cohen, from "Tower of Song"

Life After The Carnahan Affair

On December 27th, 1958, Shirley
Cavanaugh married surveyor and
adventurer John H. Garretson. She
became, finally, Shirley Garretson,
sloughing off the old life for a new hope.
On June 22nd, 1960, Shirley and John
had their first child together, and named
him Forrest Dorsey Garretson III.[47]

Shirley and John Gerretson

Shirley and Forrest Gerretson

[John Garretson personal collection]

[John Garretson personal collection]

Photographs from this era[48] were well-labeled and included
dates and names. And from 1959 to 1961, when no longer
reduced to a sensationalized headline, Shirley looked incredibly
happy …

---

[47] After John's father and brother.

[48] Obtained from John Garretson's personal collection.

After a lifetime of trauma, violence, loss, abandonment. After all the orphanages, the parental abuse and neglect. After her marriage to Walter was cut short to 10 days so he could fight in a foreign war. After the loss of so many children. So much love, betrayed. After the *entire* Pittsburgh Police Bureau tried to tear her down. After Slusser, Maloney, and Judge Harry M. Montgomery tried to put her away indefinitely. After Carnahan.

[John Garretson personal collection]

After all of it … A momentary exhale, a family, a child. Even a visit to Kennywood Park.[49]

[John Garretson personal collection]

A calming breath.

Before the fires consumed her — again.

---

[49] An amusement park located in West Mifflin, Pennsylvania.

In 1962, Shirley and John suffered the miscarriage of their second pregnancy. Soon thereafter, Forrest became sick and was diagnosed with leukemia.

John decided to move Forrest where he could get the help he needed, ultimately settling on Fort Myers, Florida. There, Forrest could get consistent treatment at Lee Memorial Hospital, a hospital renowned, at the time, for their treatments of childhood leukemia.

But Shirley did not join them, moving instead to Cleveland, Ohio, where she spent the remainder of her living days ... [50]

As with Walter, the same outcome occurred for John: their resentments were earned. Their hearts were broken by someone whose own heart, by this point in her life, must have barely fit back together.[51]

John, Forrest, and Shirley had one final gathering as a family in October of 1963, when John and Forrest flew to Ohio to visit her.

---

[50] All of the addresses listed for Shirley during these years are, I assume, various hotels and flophouses. Google maps indicate none of her Ohio addresses exist any longer. Cleveland State University Krenzler Field now sits on E 19th St. where Shirley lived. Two more of her addresses, 1858 East 29th St and 1858 E. 20th St., are now a highway. Etc.

[51] I think of the Japanese concept of *kintsugi*, where one may repair something that is broken by mending the cracks with gold. The word itself translates to golden joinery or golden repair. I do not understand the Japanese language in any manner that would allow me to functionally play with their etymologies, however, when I think of a way to change the word *kintsugi* to better fit the way I see Shirley Cavanaugh's heart, I imagine the neologism *flintsugi* to be fitting. As if all the breakage was put back together by something inspiring of fire. Something that remains ignitable, volatile.

"I have no children of my own to care for anymore, but you can't take away from a woman her mother instincts," Shirley was quoted saying in 1957.

Nine months later on July 12th, 1964, Shirley gave birth to her fourth child.

A boy.

Shirley had another chance to get it right.

Only that time her "mother instincts" genuinely took hold.

She knew the best way for her to care for a child was ... to not care for them at all.

Shirley placed her newborn in the care of the hospital for adoption.

Not left in a crib, abandoned to isolation and malnutrition.

But, rather, a hospital.

A safe space where James Russell Garretson could receive the attention and care that he needed to thrive and be adopted.

He was the last child to whom Shirley would ever give birth.

The Final Days of Shirley Cavanaugh

Tragically, the only way the remainder of Shirley Cavanaugh's life could be traced was through Cleveland police reports and St. Vincent Charity Hospital records. [1] [2] [3] [4]

On July 3rd, 1967, Shirley was admitted to St. Vincent Charity Hospital in Cleveland with chest pains, fever, and chills. Her diagnosis: chronic alcoholism, suppurative pneumonia, left-side lung abscess. According to the hospital records it was apparent that Shirley had, recently, been beaten by someone.[52]

On March 9th, 1968, Shirley was arrested for intoxication.

On May 26th, 1969, Shirley was admitted to St. Vincent Charity Hospital once more. Her body had been badly beaten, again. The official hospital record stated, "Ms. Garretson reports having fallen down a flight of stairs."

On June 12th, 1969, Shirley was admitted to St. Vincent Charity Hospital in a comatose state. Brought by a neighbor who was concerned because Shirley had been "asleep for 3 days," Shirley presented with decerebrate posturing[53] and a subdural hematoma caused by the May 26th "fall."

During the month of July 1969, Shirley spent much of her time recovering at her brother's house in Pittsburgh, during which time her 16-year-old daughter Ruth and 19-year-old daughter Judy visited her, unexpectedly.

---

[52] Family narrative suggested that, in 1968, Shirley flew to Florida to spend time with her mother Alma and step-father Chuck Hall, who had moved to Cape Coral, Florida in 1964 for Alma's health. [5]

[53] "Decerebrate posturing involves a reflex movement of muscle groups throughout your body, causing your limbs to extend and hold rigidly. These movements can happen automatically when there's severe damage to your brain or major disruptions in brain function." [5]

On September 18th, 1970, and August 16th, 1971, Shirley was arrested for intoxication and contempt of court.

On October 31st, 1972, Shirley was admitted yet again to St. Vincent Charity Hospital in Cleveland. Her admission notes read, "... severe generalized weakness and anorexia lasting for two months, severe weight loss, distending belly, jaundice skin, laennec's cirrhosis. Emergency Contact on hospital records, Mother Elmer Hall [sic] at 1613 Gardenia Blvd Fort Myers Fl."

On November 7th, 1972, Shirley Virginia Cavanaugh, Lauterbach, Garretson died of cirrhosis at the age of 44.[54]

---

[54] Her final hospital notes were explained to me by family friend and nurse practitioner Ash Kehoe: "Cirrhosis of the liver without hepatitis. Which is inflammation of the liver. Cause of the liver failure likely due to alcohol. Last line is hepatic coma and failure. So it looks like she died of liver disease, her liver was scarred (cirrhosis) from alcohol. When our livers are scarred they can't remove the toxins and we develop something called encephalopathy, which is a term for general disease of the brain. In liver failure the toxins build up and we get confused, our kidneys can't manage the toxins and eventually we can't wake up anymore."

The soul departed in the Lord does not die; it returns to God, who is the Giver of life

In Loving Memory of

Shirley Garretson

Died November 7th, 1972

⚓ HE LORD is my shepherd I shall not want. He maketh me to lie down in green pastures; He leadeth me beside the still waters. He restoreth my soul. He leadeth me in the path of righteousness for His name's sake. Yea though I walk through the valley of the shadow of death, I will fear no evil; for Thou art with me; Thy rod and Thy staff they comfort me. Thou preparest a table before me in the presence of mine enemies. Thou anointest my head with oil; my cup runneth over. Surely goodness and mercy shall follow me all the days of my life; and I will dwell in the house of the Lord forever.

___

ZORN & LUCAS Funeral Home
Braddock, Pa.

SHIRLEY GARRETSON
Shirley Cavanaugh Garretson of Cleveland, (formerly of Braddock), died last Tuesday, November 7th.

The daughter of Charles E. and Alma Hall, she was the sister of Audrey Caspero, Frank Cavanaugh, Charles H. and George W. Hall.

Friends were received at the Zorn-Lucas Funeral Home, 445 Fourth St., Braddock, where the Rev. M. Blaine Simon of the Bethel Lutheran Church officiated at services Saturday, Nov. 11 at 10 a.m. Interment was in Monongahela Cemetery.

Zorn & Lucas Funeral Home
445 FOURTH STREET
BRADDOCK, PENNA. 15104

Shirley Garretson
Died Nov 7th 1972

55

___

[55] Thanks to Elsa Horensky, Ruth's adoptive mother, for saving a lock of hair, this obituary, and one of Shirley's funeral cards in an envelope.

[1] Cleveland Police Department General Records Division / Cleveland Municipal Court – Criminal Journal / Earle B. Turner, Clerk. Case Disposition Sheet. Case CR 184966, Cr 184966.

[2] Dr. Rogoff M.D. Medical/Surgical Notes for Shirley Garretson. St. Vincent Charity Hospital, Cleveland Ohio. Admitted June 20, 1967, discharged July 6, 1967.

[3] Dr. Ryan M. D. Medical/Surgical Notes for Shirley Garretson. St. Vincent Charity Hospital, Cleveland Ohio. Admitted June 12, 1969, discharged June 24, 1969.

[4] Dr. Veloso M. D. Discharge Summary for Shirley Garretson. St. Vincent Charity Hospital, Cleveland Ohio. Admitted October 31, 1972, expired November 11, 1972.

[5] Cleveland Clinic Medical. "Decerebrate Posturing." Cleveland Clinic, my.clevelandclinic.org/health/symptoms/24968-decerebrate-posturing.

"The voice of the hidden waterfall
And the children in the apple-tree
Not known, because not looked for
But heard, half-heard, in the stillness
Between two waves of the sea."

T.S. Eliot, from "Little Gidding"

Part Two: An Unjust Coincidence

Born in 1928, Shirley Cavanaugh experienced life as an ocean of extreme waves chaotically beating beneath one hurricane after another until her tragic death in 1972.

But she made an impact.

She moved the city of Pittsburgh to collective empathy. Her testimonies brought corrupt police to trial. She was a sex worker. An aspiring archeologist. She was a victim of immeasurable abuses. She was complex.

And she was a mother.

And, as this book is, ultimately, an exercise in healing generational trauma, it would be incomplete without understanding the generations that followed and what impact Shirley continued to have for decades after her death.

Born and raised apart from each other, Shirley had four living children: Judy, Ruth, Forrest, and Jim, her distributaries rippling through time. Her genes reached through the decades, flowing from the rivers of her life choices.

How did they fare?

Did those waves find stillness? Peace? Healing?

Did Shirley's children live their lives as she lived hers?

Here, the rivers and the canyons they carved through the next 50 years can be observed.

And it started — with Jim.

James Russell Garretson

On July 12th, 1964, James Russell Garretson was the last-born child of Shirley Cavanaugh. Unique amongst his siblings, on the day of his birth, Jim was placed in the care of the hospital for adoption, and was thereafter taken into foster care by the Zickefoose family, who officially adopted him on June 18th, 1968.

Jim's time with the Zickefoose family was often perilous. His adoptive mother was not only verbally abusive and struggled with alcoholism, but also kept his adoption a secret.

And his adoption remained a secret until the 1970s when Jim, coincidentally, found the first bit of evidence that suggested he might have been someone else's child: on the inside cover of one of his forgotten baby scrapbooks, Jim found the name "Shirley Garretson."

After some time had passed, and Jim aged, he went in search of any and all information he could find on the name that haunted him from his childhood scrapbook.

When he questioned his family members, Jim quickly inferred that this was the name of his birth mother. His adoption was something that could no longer be kept hidden, so, at the age of 28, Jim began his fight for all of the records he could acquire. Unfortunately, more often than not, Jim found himself hitting dead ends. His name was Zickefoose and his birth certificate reflected that ... not Garretson, and not Cavanaugh. How could he prove to anyone that these records were rightfully his to explore?

These setbacks only inspired Jim to increase his dedication. Repeatedly he went to the Cleveland municipal court, wearing a suit and tie, and carrying a briefcase, with his hair always cut professionally. Waiting until the right moment and waiting for — the right person.

Eventually Jim found them: Judge Donelly. About Donelly Jim stated:

> "I figured out his schedule. Each day at the same time I would wait outside of his chambers dressed sharp and looking professional. I came to learn the exact time he would leave his chambers daily to get a snack from the vending machine. So I'd wait for that moment. As soon as he'd come out I'd say, 'Judge Donelly, do you mind if I ask you a couple of questions between here and the vending machine? I don't want to waste your time.'"

Judge Donelly was receptive and allowed Jim to walk with him, asking questions as they went. Jim presented to Judge Donnelly his birth certificate and the name Shirley Garretson. Jim explained that the information on his birth certificate was a lie, that he knew he was adopted and pleaded for any help he could get to find more information. But without the knowledge of Shirley's power of attorney, there was little Judge Donelly could offer.

Jim, undeterred, returned to Donelly's chambers weekly for their vending machine walk. Constantly Jim presented new information, new reasons, and new evidence that he was the son of Shirley Garretson. He reassured Donelly that he had no intentions of giving up:

> "A few weeks of this and Donelly knows I'll never stop. One day I get this phone call from the court: 'Jim Zickefoose?' I said, 'Yeah?' and the voice on the other end said, 'Judge Donelly has taped a piece of paper to the right side of the reception desk near the main entrance for you.' And they hung up.

I jumped in my car and did the 45 minute drive in 25 minutes. When I arrived I walked up to the desk and this security guard stopped me, asked for my ID, and when I showed him, he pointed to the paper taped to the desk, tells me, 'That's for you.' Then he just walks away. I grabbed the note and all it said was:

John Garretson, Cape Coral, Florida."

Accordingly Jim, then, hired a private detective who quickly uncovered Garretson's phone number. Jim called John immediately.

Jim: Hello? Is this John Garretson?
John: Yes?
Jim: Did you know a woman named Shirley Garretson?
John: ...
Jim: Hello?
John: Yeah, I knew Shirley. Why call about her?
Jim: I think she may have been my mother.
John: ... Really sorry, but she died in 1972.
Jim: ...
John: Lemme ask you, when is your birthday?
Jim: July 12th, 1964.

Garretson was open, receptive, and recalled his last meeting with Shirley in October 1963.

John: Well ... I guess that makes me your dad. You're in Ohio I'm guessing?
Jim: Yes, Cleveland.
John: I think you should come down to Florida, visit, let's meet.

Without hesitation, Jim accepted and began planning for a trip to Florida to meet his father for the first time. As if this wasn't big enough, Garretson opened Jim's world in a way he hadn't anticipated. John not only told him about his mother but also ...

> **John:** ... you have siblings. One full brother, he died from leukemia when he was seven. You also have two sisters. One in Pittsburgh and one in Portland.

Jim was no longer alone, he had siblings, his father, and he knew his mother's name.

From there, Jim broadened his search.

Already having hired a private detective to find John, Jim gave him as much information as John had regarding Jim's two sisters Ruth and Judy.

Ruth's phone numbers were publicly listed and easily accessible — so Jim called one.

And on July 11th, 1996, for the first time in his life, Jim heard his sister's voice say ...

"Hello?"

Ruth Alma Cavanaugh

Ruth Alma Cavanaugh was born into an immediately tumultuous situation. Her mother, Shirley, was single, in poverty, without access to any kind of supportive resources, and, after repeated attempts and multiple jobs, was unable to afford the care that Ruth needed.

A repeat customer at The Carrie Furnace canteen, one of Shirley's waitressing jobs, gave her the solution: a brothel (under the paid-off protection of the Pittsburgh Police), where Shirley could find solid, consistent money as a sex worker.

Unable to afford the basic needs for herself *and* her daughter, Shirley eventually agreed. Tragically and quickly, however, Shirley became lost to the distances of a world far from the child for whom she was trying to provide ...

And on November 27th, 1953, Shirley's mother, Alma, found Ruth alone, in her crib, malnourished and dehydrated. Alma rushed infant Ruth to Braddock General Hospital, where she would remain until December 13th, 1953. Her one-month birthday. [1]

Upon admittance, at two weeks old, Ruth weighed only four and a half pounds.[56]

When she was discharged, Shirley was nowhere to be found.

Ruth's care was then split between Shirley's friends, Shirley's mother, Alma, and Alma's biological brother and sister-in-law, Art and Elsa Horensky, until February of 1955 — the moment when Shirley became ensnared by policeman Eugene Coon.

From February to May of 1955, while Shirley sat in the county jail for an assault and prostitution charge Ruth's adoption was

---

[56] The average weight for a two-week-old infant girl is 8.8 pounds. [2]

brought into focus. Everyone who was aware of the situation insisted she be kept in the family and not lost to the system. Having no real stake in the matter other than their desire to be helpful and loving, Art and Elsa Horensky adopted Ruth and raised her as their own child.

On April 5th, 1955, her birth certificate was signed by the Director of Health R.F. Mathias and retro-dated to November 13th, 1953, Ruth's birthday. Her name, however, was written differently; from that day forward she was known as Ruth Elsa Horensky. [3]

Ruth Elsa Horensky birth certificate

[Personal collection]

On May 12th, 1955, Shirley was released on probation. Enmeshed in criminality, her position as Carnahan's "stool pigeon" was solidified.

Shirley would not find her way back to Ruth for as long as she lived.

Elsa Horensky, Art Horensky, Ruth Elsa Horensky

[Personal collection]

167

[1] Dr. Lowrie M.D. Medical/Surgical Notes for Ruth Alma Cavanaugh. Braddock General Hospital. Admitted Nov 27, 1953, discharged Dec 13, 1953.

[2] Whelan, Corey (Medically Reviewed By Karen Richardson Gill, MD) "What's the Average Baby Weight by Month?" https://www.healthline.com/health/parenting/average-baby-weigh t July 1, 2019.

[3] Birth Certificate, Ruth Elsa Horensky. No. 274590. Commonwealth of PA Dept. of Health, Bureau of Vital Statistics. DOB: 1953 Nov. 13. FILED: 1953, Nov. 20. SIGNED: 1955 April 5.

Ruth Elsa Horensky

Ruth learned of her adoption on July 20th, 1969 at the age of 16. "The moment the men were landing on the moon," she often recounted.

> "Dad cleared his throat and just blurted it out, 'You're adopted.' He tells me, 'Your mother is still alive, she's sick and staying with her brother.' He then proceeded to describe Shirley to me. She was someone I had run into a few times as a kid. Apparently, when I was still a baby, I was passed around to all of her friends. They took care of me ..."

As Neil Armstrong took his first steps, Ruth took hers, too — her world had been blown apart on scales unimaginable. Art then proceeded to tell her about her sister, Judy.

> "I knew her! She was a waitress at a burger joint called Winky's. I remember people would always ask if she was my sister because of how much we looked alike. When I asked them why they hadn't told me before Mom looked at me and said, 'We wrote to Ann Landers, she told us not to say anything ...' Then Dad just goes silent and turns back to the TV until eventually mumbling, 'Well, this is definitely going to piss off those Russians ...' Up until that point, I had been told I was found in an orphanage."

From there, Ruth went into shock and turned her attention back to the moon landing. A few days later she gathered herself, found a phone number for the Lauterbachs, and called Judy. Judy's grandmother, Martha, answered the phone. "Can I speak to Judy?" Ruth asked. "Tell her it's her sister." After the initial shock had worn off, Martha called in Judy.

> "The phone's for you ... it's ... your sister ... Ruth."

Judy took the receiver and greeted her sister for the first time. She and Ruth talked a while and decided to meet and spend some time getting to know each other. Both of them were thrilled to learn they had sisters, and even more thrilled to learn the truth about their mother. Together they grew the courage to visit Shirley in 1969 while she was recovering in Pittsburgh. Ruth recalled:

> "She was barely coherent, in poor health, in the throes of alcoholism. I wanted to see her again, but she moved back to Cleveland soon thereafter. She died in '72. Judy and I went to the funeral home together. It was strange to see her. We were inspecting her, she looked just like Judy, we knew we'd never get another chance. We took a lock of her hair."

But Ruth was much more than just the daughter of Shirley Cavanaugh.

Backstage Disco at the Holiday House

Ruth came of age in the 1960s and 70s, during the era of hippies and second-wave feminism, both of which heavily influenced her personality. She was an artist. She rode motorcycles. She was a fashion expert and hairstylist.

[Personal collection]

But most prominently, Ruth was an outstanding dancer, and was often found spinning across the famous floors of The Backstage at The Holiday House in Monroeville, Pennsylvania with her partner, actor John Vargas (who was attending Carnegie Mellon University for drama).

> "During a production of *West Side Story*," Vargas stated during a phone interview, "when I had the part of Bernardo, Ruth gave me such a badass haircut, and *not* a mullet, they had her cut the hair of the entire gang of Sharks. She was that good."

About dancing with Ruth, John stated:

> "I don't know how to express how vital Ruth was to the Pittsburgh dance scene in the 70s. Now you have to know — partner dancing was still new in Pittsburgh in the 70s. What I learned growing up in the Bronx was the Latin Hustle and what I learned, I taught Ruth and she'd pick it up immediately and we would just push the limits. I built a dance floor on the roof of my apartment where we could practice until we heard mourning doves. Arthur Murray's Dance Studio used to send their best teachers to just watch her and study how she danced. Every club

171

we walked into, they cleared the floor, they gave us the best table, you can see how jealous those people are in those photos of us dancing. It was like that everywhere we went."

[Personal collection]

In 1978, as Ruth was becoming well known around the local dance halls as someone to pay attention to, she was given a teaching position at Arthur Murray's Dance Studio in downtown Pittsburgh. The same studio that would send out teachers to take notes on her and John's dancing skills.

It was there that Ruth's life would change in ways, perhaps, for which she was never made ready. Ruth met and fell in love with one of her students. A football player and electrical engineer returning from Columbia University named Bruce who, on a whim, decided to sign up for dance lessons because he wanted "to do something that scared him."

[Personal collection]

The two of them spent the last few years of the 1970s drinking vodka martinis and splitting dance floors in places such as the Pegasus Lounge, Howard Johnson's, One Park Avenue, Heaven, and, of course, Backstage at The Holiday House.

Soon the two of them were married, and Ruth Horensky became Ruth Kirin.

The two of them moved into a house in the suburbs of Monroeville, Pennsylvania and had two children.

In so doing, Ruth would change her name one final time to the only name I would ever know her by: Mom.

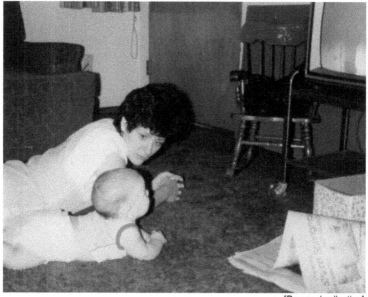

[Personal collection]

"Beautiful mother, frozen in ice
I've waited for you to grow up
for my whole life."

Poe, from "Beautiful Girl"

Ruth Elsa Kirin

[Personal collection]

My sister, Megan, was born April 3rd, 1981, and I was born 362 days later on March 31st, 1982. Truly Irish-Irish twins. By the time we were a few years old, Ruth Kirin's hair salon was no longer a dream of our mother's … It was a reality.

[Personal collection]

She was the stylist to seek out. Her ability to forecast trends in hair and clothing styles was unmatched. She made everyone she touched look and feel like a movie star.

Unfortunately, it wasn't for very long.

Over the next few years, postpartum depression coupled with mental illness made her reality nearly impossible to navigate — most days she couldn't get out of bed. Most days, she had trouble caring for us. More often than not, she had trouble caring for herself, and her hair salon was forced to close.

Our dad would walk her up and down the street daily before he went to work to get her moving. But Dad was an electrical engineer with a full-time job. He couldn't both take care of us financially and physically all day. He couldn't be in two places at once.

So, as their nature was truly a caring one, Art and Elsa, Shirley's aunt and uncle, stepped up again. As they did with our mother, so too they did for Megan and me. For the first few years of our lives, we spent most of our time in their care. They were two people for whom my sister and I have lasting love and respect. They were caring, nurturing, and truly the grandparents we needed.[57]

---

[57] Art passed away in 1999, Elsa passed in 2008.

Mom, me, Megan, Grandma and Pap-Pap

[Personal collection]

And then — a spark in the dark.

In the mid-to-late '80s, Mom became lucid and turned her efforts to circumventing depression by focusing herself on the myriad responsibilities available to being a suburban housewife and for much of our childhood, she became present. She acted against the patterns and the influence of trauma and genetics. She became an exceptionally focused mother. She organized Easter egg hunts and flea markets for the local church. She hand-sewed our Halloween costumes yearly. She cut every neighborhood kid's hair for free in our basement. She cared for every stray animal. In the 1990s, she took an interest in the new wave of home computers and started her own second hand computer hardware store. She taught me how to dance. She bought for me my first set of juggling balls. She taught me how to maintain a slick pompadour. She taught me every single call back line for The Rocky Horror Picture Show. She was smart. She was an artist.

She was good at being who she was.

But I never truly believed she was meant to live in the suburbs and be a housewife.

In retrospect I could see depression, and panic attacks, repressed, just below her surface.

As she aged alongside church gatherings, sports events, and flea markets, it was obvious that she carried an emptiness with her that could only have been filled by something that was always at arm's length.

What little she knew of Shirley and her family was no secret to us. She openly spoke of her difficulties in carrying the emptiness brought upon her by her abandonment and early childhood traumas.

Even without modern research, Mom was aware that these traumas impacted her decision-making throughout her entire life.

She carried a family-shaped hole within her heart, a blank space that we Kirins never could quite fill for her.

She was missing something.

And a phone call from Uncle Jim in 1996 began to fill it in.

Judy Louise Lauterbach

Judy and Shirley at Lauterbach Home

[Shirley's personal collection]

There were three threads that knit Judy's story together. The first and second were the family narratives of the Lauterbachs and Cavanaughs. The third was, undeniably, what held them together: Judy's profoundly self-reflective writings regarding Shirley, the Lauterbachs, and her own genetics.[58]

This book is their loom; this chapter, her tapestry.

> "I was not born without original sin," Judy wrote, "according to God most babies come into this world pure and without sin. Most, that is, except for the pitiful few unfortunates who sneak past the lord with "bad blood" gestating to wreak havoc on the world. Genetically predisposed to insanity, depravity, passion."

Judy and Shirley at Lauterbach Home

[Shirley's personal collection]

On March 30th, 1950, Judy Louise Lauterbach was born to parents Shirley and Walter Lauterbach. As an infant, Judy, for reasons that remain opaque to this day, had been abandoned by Shirley.

What were the extenuating circumstances? How much of Shirley's childhood trauma factored into her behavior? Had she simply followed the only paths she had learned to walk throughout her life?

---

[58] Reprinted here with the expressed permission of Judy's family.

Paths many of her loved ones had led her down?

It is difficult to say. For Judy, however, there was always a simple explanation for her mother's absence:

> "I had been abandoned. For some reason being given this, although limited, information at the age of seven or eight, it becomes diluted. Too young to realize its true impact yet young enough to relegate it to the massive sphere of experiences and information being imprinted on the psyche."

Judy understood how her trauma lived within.

Trauma so deeply imprinted upon her that Judy would be moved by it for her entire life.

Her developmental years were spent living with her father, Walter and her grandmother, Martha, in Wilkinsburg.

> "I was lucky. At least I knew people who had known and seen my mother. [But at] that point in my life I hadn't given much thought to my blood, or why Dad and I called the same woman 'Mum ...'"

While both Judy and Walter called Martha "Mum," having someone to call "Mum" did not mitigate what Judy had already begun to have "imprinted on her psyche." And the impact of the emptiness left by Shirley was palpably unsettling to everyone in the family. Judy painted a chillingly vivid image of the photographs of Shirley she had found around her house — explaining just how palpable it was ...

> "... all the photos with smooth feminine hands protectively entwined around the baby fat folds of my arms or legs were unfailingly accompanied by a gaping void where angry scissors desperately eliminated the

woman's image. Successful in eradicating her identity while boldly revealing the inconsolation of Mum's anger and Dad's pain. Thin, fragile fingers with, I imagined; luminously colored fingernails, small roman sandaled feet and no face. Such a small wisp of a presence for such large gaping intentional screaming holes. Not until I was solemnly and ceremoniously informed about my blood did I realize — the intentional void in the photos was the source of my unfortunate fate."

While Shirley's absence was met with very reasonable resentment by the Lauterbachs, Judy was still able to see her through a more innocent and empathetic lens. Through all of her trauma and lingering resentment, her heart was open to her mother:

"What the Lauterbach's new daughter-in-law, sister-in-law, wife etc. had survived to this point in her life was inconceivable to them. They could not have imagined the horrors Shirley had endured prior to her entering their lives. Even by today's standards it is difficult to conceive of. The very worst of what [we] knew of her was the very least of what there was to know."

Judy with half-siblings

[Lauterbach family collection]

182

At some point, Walter remarried and moved with Judy and his wife to Turtle Creek, Pennsylvania, where, over the next few years, Judy would gain three half-siblings. In a 1996 interview, Judy expressed not only her fondness for her new family, but also her feeling of disconnection from them. Judy was much older than her half-siblings and often felt like the outcast of the family.

Judy with half-siblings

[Lauterbach family collection]

She wasn't wrong. Judy was unique among her half-siblings not simply because of the gap in their ages, but also because Judy was forced to carry the troubling weight of abandonment and genetics.

By her teenage years, Judy began to show signs of mental illness. Her behavior became more erratic, unpredictable, and concerning to her family:

> "There were trouble signs. I'd have to be watched closely and kept on a short leash. [Remember] I have her blood. It's bad blood."

Consequently, as a teenager, Judy was moved back to Wilkinsburg to live with her grandparents throughout high school.

During these years, Judy was known to take an interest in art and writing, and worked as a waitress at Winky's, a popular Pittsburgh burger franchise.

But in 1969, Judy's life took a thrillingly personal 90-degree turn and opened an unanticipated path. At home with her grandmother in Wilkinsburg, the Lauterbach's landline began to ring.

From the other room, Judy heard her grandmother answer, gasp deeply and pause for an uncharacteristically long time before saying, "Judy, the phone's for you ... it's ... your sister ... Ruth."

Judy was elated and for the next few years she and Ruth would be able to share a period of their lives as siblings in close proximity. Upon graduating high school, however, Judy moved to Portland, Oregon and began a life of independence, making her connection to her sister consistently subluxed and difficult to maintain.

Judy returned home, briefly, in 1972, where she and Ruth, together, attended their mother's viewing. Left alone with Shirley resting in her casket, Judy and Ruth spent a few moments in investigative disbelief. They lifted blankets, peeked at her features, and even cut off a lock of her hair.

"It was almost as if we were inspecting her because we knew we'd never get another chance," Judy stated, "and I looked at her face and I thought, 'Why, she looks just like me!'" [1]

Judy Lauterbach and Ruth Kirin

[Personal collection]

But Judy couldn't stay for the service. Instead, she slipped out and returned to Portland. Her next visit to Pittsburgh would be in 1980, for Ruth's wedding.

Elsa Horensky. Judy Lauterbach. Bruce Kirin. Ruth Kirin. Art Horensky. Audrey and Bob Caspero.

59

[Personal Collection]

---

[59] I always appreciated that Shirley's sister, Audrey, was present for Mom's wedding.

185

And while they remained in loose touch throughout the years, it was in 1996 that their lives took a mutual turn.

On July 11th, 1996, Judy's phone rang like it was 1969.

The voice on the other end said, "Hey, Jude, it's Ruth …

… I just got off the phone with our brother …"

[1] Carpenter, Mackenzie. "The Cop and the Call Girl, The Legacy of a Pittsburgh Shooting: A Family Pulls itself Together." *Pittsburgh Post-Gazette*, 4 Aug. 1996, Sun. P. 1, 14 and 15. https://www.newspapers.com/image/90048727

Forrest Dorsey Garretson III
June 22nd, 1960 - January 24th, 1967

My dear Forrest,

In 1967, you died as a child, 15 years before I became one myself. Leukemia. Awful. I read your autopsy report a few weeks ago. I am sorry that you had to experience that. I am sorry that your short time here was rampant with such hardships. Today, looking at photos of you, John, and Shirley, having a momentary life of joy — I see your story clearly.

Shirley Garretson, John Garretson, Forrest Garretson

[John Garretson personal collection]

You were ephemeral love, a flash of light in a world too often overshadowed by darkness.

Your mother had a difficult life. At the same time you were diagnosed with leukemia, Shirley suffered a miscarriage. After all that happened to her in life until that point, all she could do was run. She fled for safety. Collapsed her life before life could collapse her. She left you to be raised as an only child and only as a child. It wasn't your fault. Nothing was.

As Shirley disappeared over the horizon, your father dedicated what little time he had left with you to keeping you healthy, happy, and loved.

Even by the age of six, you made an impact in certain people's lives. Not the least of which was your first grade class, each of whom wrote you a letter saying they missed you. They each drew a picture of themselves with their arms open, hoping and wishing you would come back to school soon.[60]

---

[60] Obtained from John Garretson's personal collection

But you never did. You never had a chance to finish your first-grade workbooks. Even though you lived your complete story I can't help but wonder what potential chapters would have awaited you. I can't help but dream about the character you would have become.

One of my favorite discoveries about you was something I found printed in the *Fort Myers News Press* about one month after your death.

The Fort Myers Library had a fine-free week; it gave people the opportunity to return all of their late books without incurring any penalties. Your childhood dentist, Dr. W. B. Dehon, made a donation of $20 for a memorial book in your name.

Now, my dear uncle, there are two books out there that carry with them your memory.

Library Gets Overdue Books

The Fort Myers Library's recent fine-free week brought in a total of 53 long overdue books, Mrs. R. P. Norton, librarian, told the board Tuesday.

She said the January circulation of 12,084 volumes was an increase of 598 over the previous January and that the December, 1966, circulation of 10,541 was a 1,364 increase over the same month the previous year.

New registrations during the past two months totaled 239. Monday night's circulation for December and January hit 1,107.

Gifts of $20 from Dr. W. B. Dehon were reported for memorial books for Rhondasu Norris and Forrest Garretson.

Fort Myers News Press Wed, Feb 15, 1967

Your childhood smile will shine through the decades in the heart of these pages.

You will never be forgotten. Especially not by those who read this book.

But Forrest, I have the most exciting news to share with you …

Against all odds — your siblings found each other!

And in 1996, they came together and decided to write this book.

They didn't forget you then and now, in 2023, finishing what they started, your nephew hasn't forgotten you either.

With love, Jason

Forrest Garretson gravestone and funeral card

[John Garretson personal collection]

FORREST D. GARRETSON

Funeral service for Forrest Dorsey Garretson, 6, 5238 Pocatello Ct. Cape Coral will be held Saturday at 10 a.m. from the Chapel of the Harvey Funeral Home with Rev. Robert Veley pastor of Faith United Presbyterian Church officiating.

Surviving in addition to his father, John H. Garretson are his paternal grandmother, Mrs. Marguerite Garretson, Cape Coral and maternal grandparents Mr. and Mrs. Charles Hall of North Fort Myers. Selected to serve as pallbearers are John Bess, Lloyd Bess, Richard MacConnel and Jimmy Sherman. Honorary pallbearers will be C. H. Naugle and Peter Sales. Interment will be in the Memorial Gardens Cemetery.

Fort Myers News-Press,
26 Jan 1967, Thu. Page 2

Forrest Dorsey Garretson III, 15 months old, 1961

Forrest Dorsey Garretson III, four years old, 1964

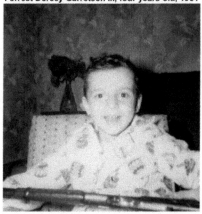

Forrest Dorsey Garretson III, six years old, 1966

"Out of suffering have emerged
the strongest souls; the most
massive characters are seared
with scars."

Kahlil Gibran

The Unfracturing Family

Judy Lauterbach, Jim Garettson, Ruth Kirin

[Personal collection]

Jim did it. In 1996, he united a fractured family and set them on a new trajectory and an unexpected adventure. Together for the first time, as Shirley Cavanaugh's children, Jim, Judy, and Ruth set out to make up for their many lost years. They grew to know each other quickly and intimately. And they did so by working to uncover the legacy of, and truth about, their mother. Each one of them took careful time to contribute what information and abilities were unique to them.

Jim had uncovered Shirley's medical and legal records from Cleveland, and his own adoption records.

Jim also found Shirley's second husband, his father, and his sisters. Jim brought the Cavanaugh children together for the first time, uniting something untied and splintered across both space and time.

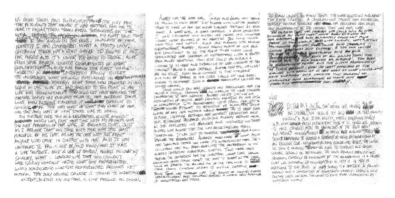

Judy had not only dedicated herself to handwriting the most poignant prose regarding the memory of Shirley, but also created a timeline on graph paper that spanned the entirety of Shirley's life.

"If I had grown up being more concerned with where I came from than where I was going, this tribute to my mother may never be written," Judy scrawled across a blank page, "... spending one's resources searching where they came from can suck the life out of seeing where to go from here ..."

And yet, still, she wrote. She spent her resources and searched with her siblings.

"As far as I can tell, our mother has haunted all of her children," Judy continued. "The ones who knew of her and the ones previously without a clue to her identity. Merely identifying Shirley has never been enough for those of us fortunate enough to have stumbled upon the parameters of the truth about our mother.

Knowing of Shirley was an obstacle, but knowing who Shirley was, seems comparable to pledging a fraternity or vying for membership at an exclusive club. Misunderstanding evolves into secrets. The closer we come to knowing her, the more the shrouds and smokescreens descend on her memory. The truth remains nebulous and guarded.

Certainly the difference of the generations is a factor. What was shameful or misunderstood in 1957 is in 1999 anathema to the truth. In 1957 Shirley is a prostitute, a fallen woman, and a caricature *of* everything unholy.

196

Nearly a half century later we peel the onion to find pure victimization *by* everything unholy."

Since Mom had been raised within the Cavanaugh/Horensky family unit, she was able to uncover nearly every photograph of Shirley that remained in the family's possession.

She, too, took time to write out as much as she could. She brought Jim, for the first time, to his mother's grave.

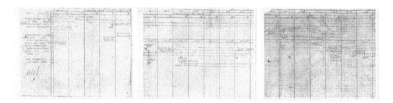

My father also created a timeline spanning across stapled-together graph paper, where he noted the chronological details of everything that they talked about. On the back of many of Shirley's press photos, he marked the date the photo was published.

My parents also gave Jim a niece and nephew who would both grow to be proud to have him as their uncle.

Megan Kirin, Ruth Kirin, James Garretson, Bruce Kirin, Jason Kirin, Corky (the Collie)

[Personal collection]

1996 - 1999 "The Shirley Cavanaugh Story"
(The Book That Was Never Written)

The Cavanaugh kids knew what needed to be done: aggregate their research and publish *The Shirley Cavanaugh Story* once and for all. And if they were going to do this research correctly and get the story straight — they were going to do it thoroughly and with a professional.

Ruth Kirin, James Garretson, Judy Lauterbach

[Personal collection]

Their first point of action was contacting four-time Pulitzer Prize nominee, *Pittsburgh Post-Gazette* journalist Mackenzie Carpenter.[61]

For a few weeks, Carpenter and the Cavanaugh kids took to libraries and archives. In partnership, they ultimately compiled their research into the 1996 article "The Cop and the Call Girl, The Legacy of a Pittsburgh Shooting: A Family Pulls Itself Together." [1]

A front-page story with a double full-page spread that read like a true crime, noir exposé, detailed The Carnahan Affair and the lives of Shirley's children, who were bonded by the lies and trauma of their shared, yet simultaneously separated, pasts.

After the article was written we all (except Judy) flew to Florida to meet, for the first time, John Garretson. We were also fortunate enough to spend time on our trip with the remaining Halls and Cavanaughs still living in Fort Myers, Florida.

Garretson was an incredibly kind man who let us stay in his home. He brought us morning coffee and regaled us with tales of his many adventures, including having walked the Appalachian Trail despite having an incredibly unbalancing limp from contracting polio earlier in life. He also told us of his travels in India and shared with us his photographs from hiking through foreign countries. He also let us know that after Forrest died he moved to Alaska and worked as a surveyor helping build the Trans-Alaska Pipeline System.

During this family reunion, I witnessed, in my mom's face, how complete Fort Myers made her. She found people who knew her mother. People she could finally connect with and feel accepted by. She was on the beach. In constant sunshine. Warmth. Hope.

She had found her family, her history.

Unfortunately — her other family had work and high school …

Our vacation came to a quick end, and as we watched Fort Myers disappear beyond the width of the airplane window, I saw Mom's face change. What, at first, was great joy and acceptance became determination.

She would find her way back to her family.

No matter the cost.

Pittsburgh Post-Gazette

SUNDAY

ONE OF AMERICA'S GREAT NEWSPAPERS

$1.50
Vol. 70, No. 4

FINAL
EDITION

AUGUST 4, 1996

INSIDE
The Games

On top yesterday

■ The Dream Team woke up something after halftime and put away Yugoslavia to win the men's basketball gold medal.

■ Miguel Indurain of Spain, five-time winner of the Tour de France, added an Olympics gold medal to his accomplishments in the cycling time trial.

■ Nigeria was the surprise winner of the men's soccer gold after its victory against Argentina.

On tap today

■ The men's marathon begins at 7 a.m. About two hours later, the track meet will have ended.

■ The closing ceremonies. Six championship bouts in the boxing tournament.

The medals

	G	S	B	Tot
USA	42	32	23	97
Germany	18	16	25	59
Russia	26	20	12	58
China	16	22	12	50
Australia	9	9	20	38

Complete coverage:
Sports

TODAY

WEATHER
Mostly sunny with a warm afternoon, high 98. Low 69.
Page A-2

BUSINESS
George Becker, president of the United Steelworkers, spells out in an interview the difficult challenges facing his union and organized labor in general. PAGE E-1

WORKPLACE
Children must be teen eliminated as little as possible in the summer during mom's office, or home working hours. PAGE D-2

SPORTS
Steelers most off a late three by the Rams to win 16-13. PAGE B-1

MAGAZINE
What started as a simple idea for giving Pennsylvania a cradle of the Turnpike has taken a few shared twists and turns. PAGE M-1

STYLEWISE
It's fine to be cool, especially where your eyes are concerned. PAGE N-1

ESSENTIALLY PITTSBURGH
They're taught to making rapid, level-movement skills and as members of the River Rescue Motorcycle Club to train hard to properly cycle safely. PAGE G-1

ARTS & ENTERTAINMENT
The Pittsburgh Ballet is shoring in its mounting of a benchmark to Patrick Wolfe. PAGE K-6

BOOKS
Pick a mystery, any mystery. PAGE H-8

FOOD
There's a book of things — $5 to be exact — that you can go with leftover chicken. PAGE S-10

TRAVEL
Yukon Ho! About my day work endless stretches of pristine wilderness and prefers to will be to the centerpiece of your vacation. PAGE F-1

— By John Murphy

INDEX

Bridge	N-8	Lottery	A-2
Mathematician	A-6	Lottery	B-4
Business	E-1	Movies	K-1
Bridge	H-9	Navigator	A-2
Business	E-1	Music	K-6
Several bar	S-5	Paar Forat	A-6
Cla-r-Foot	A-18	Obituaries	B-5
Crosswords	H-8	Pro-logue	K-1
Editorials	A-2	Rosetteles	A-14
Punt	S-12	Sports	B-1
From	F-1	Scoreboard	B-5
Horoscope	A-13	Stylewise	N-1
Also the road	D-8	Travel	F-1
Instruct	A-14	TV & radio	A-6
Involvement	B-4	Views	G-1
Lawrence	A-14	Weather	A-2

CLASSIFIED ADS

Real estate	Q-1	Merchandise	B-12
Recruitment	B-13	Automotive	B-20

PLENTY TO SEE AND HEAR

Ken Counts of the North Side helps his son Kenny, 4, cover his ears during the Regatta Drag Boat Racing. They were among an estimated 55,000 people attending Regatta events yesterday. For today, the last day of the Regatta, the weather should be partly sunny with highs between 86 and 90 degrees, and a 30 percent chance of showers in the late afternoon. Schedule and story in The Region, Page B-1.

THE COP AND THE CALL GIRL

The legacy of a Pittsburgh shooting: A family pulls itself together

By Marie-anne Carpenter
Post-Gazette Staff Writer

A beautiful call girl. The handsome married-with-children client of the Pittsburgh police's vice squad. A shooting in a "tryst" nightclub with a week-old bill delivered. A cover-up.

It was labeled "the Cannavan affair," and the lurid newspaper clippings tell a tale that reads like a film noir script, but in 1967, during Shirley Cavanaugh's life, it was, during an enticement to an affair born-rich. The incident set off a scandal that had Pittsburgh readers on the edge of their review for months.

But there was another story, one that never made its way into print. This was a story about four children and their mother who, somehow, pulled out that it a brutal to cry for lives. Two girls and two boys for different old fathers grew up for almost a father of mutual to hatred, never knowing the complete truth about their past.

Until now.

Those were ago, on July 11, 1978 Sons of, at Murfreysville, joe a parent visit from a man she didn't know.

Hello, Buck, a voice said. This is your younger brother, Jim.

John, Shirley Cavanaugh's second eldest

These side-by-days of indignation as Shirley Cavanaugh walked past Lt. Allen Cannahan at a police trial board where charges were brought against Cannavan in 1967. Cavanaugh's elder son, John V. Bros, Springsteel, refused to let her testify at the hearing.

SEE RELATIVES, PAGE A-14

SEE RELATIVES, PAGE A-14

CLOSE ENCOUNTERS

They found each other, home on the rivers

This weekend, Pittsburgh celebrates the rivers that run through it with the Three Rivers Regatta. But the rivers also bring together more than their players by play. When you are a frequent visitor to a bit of former plot, reverence to the spot the rivers do along with the people who work on them. People like Carl Ross Luebil and his wife Jean, who, for many years, spent much more time on the water than they did on land.

By Bob Betz Jr.
Post-Gazette Staff Writer

Stanley Luebil fell into working on the rivers, and wound up making them his life.

It was in his Robinson man technically is retold as a riverboat pilot, but he still works on occasional trips having quit his

served his riparian pilot's license for this many years. The role that primarily provides the father to "Captain" As silent he says. "This is Carl, then."

His career started 45 years ago when he was growing up in Kennard, W.Va., on the Ohio River above the Pittsburgh.

"Your Luck, Lt." Luebil said, placing it the way up the river out then.

His Polish immigrant mother had moved him and his five sisters three after their father was killed in a coal mine accident in 1949. The Depression infected them.

Luebil remembers one of nine sisters an aged broken-from a bed to say family the river to the years mentioned since time the luck will. Legendally Jimmy Bill name

one of the boathouse and woke him with a swift kick in the butt.

"Get up, Get up mate there, Rieslig," Luebil would add a grin. "He did so called out 'Yesug.' Get Jesus down in that boat and go to work!"

The boat was the STB, steamest S.B. Stahl. Like the other boys then plying the rivers, he was a big jackleutender, propelled by a paddlewheel at her stern. And

SEE RIVERS, PAGE A-12

SEE RIVERS, PAGE A-12

ANALYSIS

Parties bicker over record

Did late spurt make up for Congress' stalemate for most of this session?

By Helen Dewar and Eric Pianin
The Washington Post

WASHINGTON — Democrats don't have a '96 nothing' Congress to kick around anymore, After the Republicans pushed the nation's attention to turning a government shutdown in their budget war with President Clinton, Democrats were mapping plans to run against the GOP majority for failing to do anything except enact tax cuts.

But now in a frenzy of lawmaking before leaving for its month-long summer break, the GOP-controlled 104th Congress won Clinton's approval for a radical overhaul of welfare and passed bills to expand access to health insurance, raise the minimum wage, cut lobbyists' taxes and quicken drinking water rules. That came on top of earlier action to reshape farm programs and telecommunications law.

Was it enough just enough, Congress down final action making illegal immigration, overhauling control programs, revising terrorism and addressing other high-profile expenses that divide while the law is Americans before the November elections.

"We've moved from a very difficult phase to a very positive phase," said House Republican Conference Chairman John A. Boehner, R-Ohio.

There are varieties of reasons for this. When historic Majority Leader Trent Lott, R-Miss., took over to talk June from Bob Dole, who had three principal for months with his presidential campaign, Lott started smoking the whip and forcing a resolution of important that had been tying up much more legislation.

Perhaps more significantly, Some GOP leaders, chastened by a public backlash against last year's two governmental shutdowns,

SEE CONGRESS, PAGE A-8

SEE CONGRESS, PAGE A-8

Fears cause U.S. to order dependents to leave Saudi base

By Bradley Graham and R. Jeffrey Smith
The Washington Post

WASHINGTON — Defense Secretary William Perry said yesterday to respond to new terrorist attacks against U.S. forces in the Persian Gulf, and his decision ordered about 760 military dependents and their active-age students to leave Saudi Arabia.

"We are not ordinary forces in Saudi Arabia under terrorist attack," Perry told a group of defense writers. "We expect more terrorist attacks."

According to Air raid, U.S. forces based on the recent attacks on the highest state of alert, after than 4,500 troops are being moved to a remote site which at the Saudi capital of Riyadh, and options and children will be ought be allowed to accompany most Defense Department personnel stationed at small Arabia.

"We are taking some extraordinary measures to protect our military personnel," Perry said in an interview in his Pentagon offices.

Perry noted plans a number of candidates that he made Friday in an interview with National Public Radio. In that interview, he said that any "property" behind the June 25 bombing that killed 19 airmen in Dhahran, and that the Saudis were expected to keep up their investigations on the base Saudi.

He said that he would not be based on direct knowledge that was behind the attack, and that the only direct to say that the attack's complete nature and the size of the truck bomb explosion pointed to "evidence of international terrorism."

The Saudis have made statements about their intentions to large restraints. Perry said, noting that he was what he was referring to.

Perry said he had glossed "nothing too obvious who is responsible for the bombing" during his visit last week to Saudi Arabia. He said that he spoke of signs when he discussed the investigation on Friday to the

SEE SAUDI, PAGE A-3

SEE SAUDI, PAGE A-3

[62] Strangely, the third photo in the second row, I can confirm, is *not* a photo of Shirley Cavanaugh but of a woman named Maida Routhas who was involved in a case connected to Maloney. Apparently, Maloney was often seen at her restaurant accepting "bags of cash" as bribes from racketeers.

PITTSBURGH POST-GAZETTE ■ SUNDAY, AUGUST 4, 1996   A-15

THE STORY THAT ROCKED PITTSBURGH

Ruth Roth and her half-brother, Jim, at their first meeting July 19

204

[1] Carpenter, Mackenzie. "The Cop and the Call Girl, The Legacy of a Pittsburgh Shooting: A Family Pulls itself Together." *Pittsburgh Post-Gazette*, 4 Aug. 1996, Sun. P. 1, 14 and 15.
https://www.newspapers.com/image/90048727

Chasing Family

After we returned home from Florida, we all went back to our lives. Jim went back to Cleveland and the wave of familial elation Mom had been riding for weeks began to slow. The tides unrippled into stilled water.

The seasons changed.

Mom was home without her birth family, and the emptiness they had filled had returned in their absence. An emptiness she tried her best to fill in their stead, often with alcohol, sometimes with much harder drugs. Sometimes — with other people. The depression intensified, the panic attacks overwhelmed her, and us, weekly. Her behavior became erratic. And while she and Dad made an honest attempt at therapy, their marriage deteriorated. In 1997, their relationship crescendoed into something detrimental for the entire family — so they separated. Dad moved out of the house and into an apartment on the other side of town. Both parents bore responsibility for the divorce, and my dad acknowledged his onus in the situation. He's a brave man who owns up to the messes he made.

As a matter of convenience, Megan moved in with Dad and I stayed living with Mom …

Our family was in pieces.

Mom just said goodbye to her sister again. Her brother went back to Cleveland. Her cousins from the Hall and Cavanaugh families were in Fort Myers, Florida, over 1,000 miles away and her husband moved into an apartment across town with their daughter …

I've thought about how, when we reach our lowest and darkest points, we try to revert back to an iteration of ourselves that was most calm, most in love. We say, "I need to get back to who I was, back when I was happy."

For Mom, that place of happiness, that calm, was with her family in Fort Myers.

She wanted it back.

So we chased it.

Summer of 1997, when school let out, Mom asked me the most important question of my life:

"If you could travel anywhere in the U.S., where would you go and why?"

To a 15-year-old boy named Jason obsessed with the writings of Poppy Z. Brite — there was only one answer ...

"New Orleans," I said, "to find vampires."

Smiling slyly, Mom looked at me and said, "Let's go find some vampires then ..."

Within two days of that conversation, our bags were packed and we leapt into her gray Dodge Caravan for the local AAA to have TripTiks made.

At the counter, behind the AAA employee, was a wall of rectangular boxes in as many rows and columns as from floor to wall to ceiling would allow. Each box contained a road map roughly 3x8-inch in dimension and on the top of each map were holes to collectively bind them with a plastic spiral. Each map could be placed on top of, or beneath, any other map to connect the maps via a road. Resulting in one, spiral bound, pack of 3x8 maps that created the outline for a road trip.

Mom leaned against the counter, looked at the employee, and said, "Pittsburgh to Nashville and Memphis ..." She stuck out her fingers, cocked a hip, and started counting them off, "Memphis to Cullman, Alabama. Cullman to New Orleans. New Orleans to Fort Myers, Florida." She looked back at me and winked. "Let's go see Graceland, the Civil Rights Museum, the Grand Ole Opry, Ave Maria Grotto, South of the Border, New Orleans, Florida. Everything. Let's see it all ..."

Turning back to the employee, Mom smiled and said, "Lastly, Florida to South of The Border in South Carolina then ... South Carolina back to Pittsburgh."

Upon leaving the AAA parking lot, we'd call the local radio station to request "Free Fallin'" by Tom Petty to play us out of town.

At 15 years old, I just assumed my parents had money that I didn't. So I never asked how our trips were funded. But Dad later informed me that Mom had written bad checks and forged credit cards in his name. She bought a bunch of jewelry, which she hocked for quick cash, and we set out on our journey South.

From 1997-1999, three summers in a row, my mother and I packed ourselves, and whoever else cared to join, into that van and we drove. Fueled by NoDoz and Camel Cigarettes, we hit Memphis, the Opry, and every tourist trap along the way.

[Personal collection]

Every time there was some off-the-path billboard telling us to come pan for rocks — we couldn't resist.

We'd drive through Mississippi and complain about driving through Mississippi.

208

Grand Ole Opry, Nashville, Tennessee

[Personal collection]

When night came and we grew tired, we'd pull off into a church parking lot and sleep in the van.

Sometimes she'd buy us a six-pack and we'd sit in the van with the windows down, drink beers, and smoke cigarettes into the night.

One night, beer-drunk under a dark sky in a church parking lot, a half-broken-hearted smile shyly formed across her face. "When I am gone," she told me, sipping her beer, "and you can smell flowers where there are no flowers to be seen," another sip, "that's where I am, that's when you'll know I'm there."

We clinked our bottles together, reclined the front seats, and went to sleep.

Each morning we found the nearest Waffle House and had breakfast. We showered weekly at truck stops for $10.

Once we caught a Garth Brooks performance at the Opry on a $7 ticket. One summer, she timed our drive so that we'd witness a shuttle launch at The Kennedy Space Center in Florida.

Bienville Street and Chartres Street, New Orleans, Louisiana

[Personal collection]

On one random day, mid-summer, she dropped me at the corner of Bienville St. and Chartres St. in the French Quarter.

As she smiled from the van window, she aimed her camera at me and said, "Be back here in exactly ten hours."

Unaware of where she went or what she did, I spent the day searching for vampires.

It was all marvelous.

But every year, it was the same thing: Mom chased that feeling, that family, from 1996. And no matter where we drove, we always ended up in Florida, spending a week or so with Frankie Cavanaugh (Shirley's nephew), our cousins, John Garretson, Chuckie Hall Jr., et al.

Fort Myers Fishing Pier Beach, Florida

[Personal collection]

210

But the problem with our trips was ... they had to end. We always had to return to Pittsburgh.

And from August to May, when we were not on the road, somewhere ultimately en route to Florida, Mom worsened. The fall would arrive and, thereafter, winter would engulf everything she considered warm. She made continued attempts at new careers: once she owned a consignment shop in Monroeville, Pennsylvania. Once, she owned a café in Swissvale, Pennsylvania. Either way, the book that she and her siblings attempted to write was forgotten.

When asked what happened, Jim was quoted as saying, "Are you kidding me? Three Shirleys under one roof? We couldn't get *anything* done."

Each of them was afflicted with mental illness, drug use, alcoholism, and genetics. All during a decade where mental health care had only begun to (barely) be taken seriously or even sincerely — especially for women. Like Shirley, her children, too, lived in a society devoid of support for their needs as humans with chemical imbalances. The struggle caused the three of them to shelve their entire project and part ways in 1999.

Mom spiraled at terminal velocity.

She hardened to the world around her. She became suicidal. She had panic attacks daily. And nightly she would see closing time at the local dive bars. Throughout my high school experience, during the school year when we were not on the road, she was in and out of the psychiatric hospital every few months. When she was at home for prolonged periods of time, chaos grew within her and exploded in a rage she'd take out on the walls, objects, and people closest to her.

One night she took it out on the house itself and set a fire in the second floor bathroom closet. With a fire extinguisher in each hand and a phone cocked between shoulder and ear, I called 911 and blasted the bathroom until the canisters were empty of CO_2. The fire department arrived in time to save the first floor and basement. But the attic, where our childhood memories were stored, was entirely lost to flames and water damage. Our insurance company put us in an Extended Stay America until our house was repaired.

By the time I was 18, I prevented her suicide four or five times. I cut her down twice from makeshift nooses. Once I managed to scoop out a mouthful of Klonopin before she had time to grab water to swallow.

Her alcoholism, solitude, childhood adversity and abandonment, mental struggles, medications, nicotine addiction, genetics, and cocaine use collided with each other, and she broke from within.

As a teenager, I didn't understand what was happening, and I knew there wasn't anything I could do to help.

So I left.

"Good night New Orleans
Things are exactly as they seem,
but I'm nowhere around."

Joseph Arthur, from "Speed of Light"

2001 - 2003 Back to New Orleans

The last year and a half of high school I lived in my father's apartment with him and my sister. It was incredibly small but we made it work. Dad even took it upon himself to make a collapsible wall to bisect his bedroom. He slept on one side and I on the other.

I thought of Mom frequently, and often she would call. But our phone conversations were never easy to be a part of. They tended to be one-sided, late at night, she would call me while intoxicated, hurt, and alone. Her reality complexified mine. And at 19 years old, I had no means to relate safely to her.

I knew she was on prescription medication for Borderline Personality Disorder and was even seeing a therapist, but her drinking and drug use prevented those medications and therapy from ever being very effective.

It was not an easy world for her to exist in, and I didn't have the tools needed to even begin to help her.

In 2001, I graduated high school. Being an "adult" I decided to leave Pittsburgh altogether.

I made my way, without delay, back ... to New Orleans.

But instead of searching for vampires I sought poets, solace, and circus artists.

From 2001 - 2003, I attended the New Orleans School for the Imagination to study "Poetry as a Second Language" with Dave Brinks as my teacher. I also attended the University of New Orleans for general education.[63] I worked part time as a carpenter's assistant and part time as a porter in a bar called

---

[63] Thank you dad.

The Tricou House at 711 Bourbon St. All the while I learned many unique juggling techniques from local busking artists.

My time in New Orleans was the defining period of my life. Away from Pittsburgh, away from my family, I was myself for the first time, truly. From New Orleans, the forking paths of my life became manifold and I followed them all with abandon. I began to grow from new seeds of self. I began to see who I was for the first time.

In 2002, for my 20th birthday, I came back to Pittsburgh. Nearly three years had passed since I'd seen Mom. When I asked around to her friends, I learned she was, at the time, staying in the psychiatric ward of Forbes Regional Hospital in Monroeville, Pennsylvania.

So I visited her.

Her general demeanor was somber but lucid. Monitored by medical professionals, detoxed from alcohol, she was in a fairly coherent state. Neither of us made much eye contact, our gaze often downcast — as if there was something we both wanted to say but instead we let fear, or insecurity, hold us back.[64] We smoked a few cigarettes together. We got to smile some. We reminisced about our road trips, fallin' free down South to see family.

I told her I moved to New Orleans.

She laughed and asked, "You find the vampires?"

"No," I smiled, "unfortunately."

---

[64] The word "mamihlapinatapai" from the extinct Yaghan language of the Tierra del Fuego people is defined as "a look shared by two people expressing the desire for the same thing however neither individual is willing to initiate."

When she asked how to contact me I gave her my phone number.

I kissed her cheek and stood to leave.

"Remember the smell of flowers," she said as she put out her cigarette, "never forget the smell of flowers."

"I won't." I said, turning to leave, "... bye, Mom." [65]

I walked down the hall and was buzzed through a locked door.

A few days later, I was on a plane back to New Orleans.

On one or two more rare occasions she called me. Each time I could tell by her language, the time of night, and slurred speech she was having trouble again. The chaos growing within her.

But it was the phone call on May 13th, 2003, two days after Mother's Day, that was the last conversation we ever had.

My newly purchased Nokia began to ring ...

"Hello?" I answered, pensive.

On the other end of the line, Mom's words dragged. Her voice — cigarette smoked gravel, layered with alcohol and downers.

She was calling to tell me she loved me — to tell me that she never left my side and never would.

I told her I missed her. That I loved her.

I wished her a happy Mother's Day.

---

[65] "I am with you in Rockland." Allen Ginsberg, from "Howl."

Our conversation was brief.

I went back to work at The Tricou House, I went back to my life.

A few days later, my phone rang again.

It was my father this time calling to tell me ... Mom was dead.

On May 13th, 2003, after we had finished our phone conversation — my mother, Ruth Elsa Kirin, stepped into her bedroom closet and hanged herself.

Mom's funeral card

In Loving Memory of
RUTH ELSA KIRIN
Nov 13, 1953 - May 13, 2003

After Glow

I'd like the memory of me to be a
  happy one,
I'd like to leave an afterglow of smiles when
  day is done.
I'd like to leave an echo whispering softly
  down the ways,
Of happy times and laughing times and
  bright and sunny days.
I'd like the tears of those who grieve, to dry
  before the sun
Of happy memories that I leave behind
  when day is done.

Arrangements By
James F. Kutch Funeral Homes
East McKeesport, PA & Rankin

[Personal files]

Mom's suicide note excerpt

[Personal files]

Mom's obituary

KIRIN
RUTH ELSA (HORENSKY)
On Tues., May 13, 2003, age 48, of
Monroeville, formerly of Swissvale.
Survived by her daughter Megan Ki-
rin of Penn Hills, and son Jason Ki-
rin of New Orleans; beloved daugh-
ter of Elsa (Pesavento) Horensky
and the late Arthur Horensky of
Braddock Hills; sister of James
Zickefoose of FL and Judy Lauter-
baugh of OR; also survived by
aunts, uncle, cousins and many
friends. She will be missed by all.
No visitation. Interment will be at
Monongahela Cemetery in Brad-
dock Hills.
Please sign the guest book at post-gazette.com

[Post-Gazette archives]

Mom's suicide note excerpt

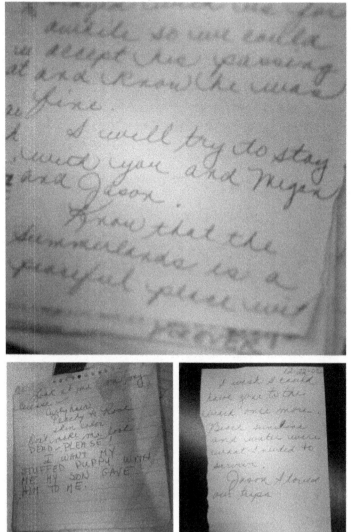

[Personal files]

"You'll live to dance another day
It's just now you'll have to dance for the two of us
So stop looking so damn depressed
And sing with all your heart — long live the queen."

Frank Turner, from "Long Live the Queen"

May 2003 - Back to Pittsburgh

I packed what little I owned into the bed of my 1991 Chevy Cheyenne pickup truck and drove back to Pittsburgh for Mom's interment. There I stood lost amongst a vague crowd. A swath of facelessness across a group of familiar people. Like white noise in the form of closeness. I specifically remember one person inching towards me as I inched away. I knew Uncle Jim was in town. I was vaguely aware of Aunt Judy's presence. I knew my father, my grandmother Elsa, my sister, and my friends must have been there.

My lucidity that day was singular: I witnessed myself as I stood, dwarfed by a vacant, colossal, grass hill, with a single gravestone in front of me that read "Shirley Garretson." Beneath her name, one word was also inscribed: Ruth.

Just ... Ruth.

With that lucidity came the profound revelation that although it took 50 years, Shirley finally found her way back to her daughter.

And no one will be able to separate them again.

[Personal collection]

The End of an Era

Over the next decade, some of my mother's belongings trickled into my possession. My sister had a box of photos and scrapbooks. My grandmother Elsa had a box of letters, childhood memorabilia, and school photos. Everyone had something. My Aunt Janet too had things to share.[66]

It's a complex and vague memory but during the shuffling of belongings — someone gave me the box that included mom's 75-page, handwritten suicide note.

In the article "The Cop and The Call Girl," Jim reflected:

> "All of Shirley's kids are being punished by something they have no control over. I missed 32 years with Judy and Ruth, and after spending one day with Ruth, I was mad that I had to wait so long to enjoy that."

All of the work the Cavanaugh kids had done, all of the photos they had uncovered, were boxed up and put into storage.

Mom recounted in that same article, "I grew up with so many secrets ... I want to find all the answers ..."

But it didn't happen.

The Cavanaugh kids never completed their research, and never compiled their book.

I knew a day would come when it would fall on me to finish what they'd started.

---

[66] Francis Cavanaugh's daughter. Shirley's niece. In connecting with her about this book, she asked me not to use her last name. She was remarkably special to me growing up. Her presence in my mother's family always brought me warmth. She is one of the babies in the photo of Shirley and Alma on page 91.

I knew I would have to wait until I was strong enough to face what was in those boxes.

I would have to be stable enough, with an appropriate support network, and therapist.

And it would be 20 years before I could make that happen.

"This is the way leaves fall around a tree in autumn, the tree unaware of the rain running down its sides, of the sun or the frost, and of life gradually retreating inward. The tree does not die. It waits."

Hermann Hesse, from "Demian"

Part Three: A Just Coincidence

Shirley Cavanaugh had four children:

Judy Lauterbach, Ruth Kirin, Forrest Garretson III, and James Garretson.

Each of their histories were cathedrals of complexity and each of their lives are a testament to genetics and to generational trauma.

By running background checks through *TruthFinder.com* I was able to uncover that, independent of each other, both Judy and Mom had charges filed against them for driving under the influence, driving with suspended licenses, and possession and trafficking of controlled substances. For Judy it was cannabis, and for Mom it was cocaine.

Furthermore, through that same site, I found that Mom had received an eviction notice on July 18th, 2002. Our childhood home had gone up for sheriff's sale.

Tragedy upon tragedy.

Loss upon loss.

Generation upon generation.

Shirley Cavanaugh had four children ...

Subsequently, she has three grandchildren.

Two of whom I have the consent to write about.

But first — I feel it is necessary to explain how this book was written.

2022 - 2023 "From The Furnace With Love"
(The Book That Was Written)

In 2022, while reading about intersectional feminism[67], I became aware of the concept of Sex Worker Exclusionary Radical Feminism, or SWERF, defined the following way:

> "Sex Worker Exclusionary Radical Feminism (SWERF) emerged as a response to Third-wave feminism's more inclusive, intersectional approach to gender inequality, and is characterized primarily by discrimination against individuals engaged in sex work. These individuals include but are not limited to prostitutes, pornography models and actors, phone sex operators, erotic dancers, and webcam performers.
>
> The argument behind SWERF ideology tends to be that sex workers, particularly those in the prostitution and pornography industries, become the victims of regular sexual objectification, exploitation, and violence; and that, by participating in this kind of industry, sex workers become co-perpetrators of these crimes.
>
> While most feminist schools support an individual's right to choose what sexual activities they do or do not engage in, SWERFs take it upon themselves to tell other people what, and what not, to do with their bodies." [1]

I immediately thought of Shirley and how I, coincidentally, am the indirect product of a sex worker. Accordingly, I reflected on my beliefs regarding sex work.

---

[67] "Intersectionality is widely used to illustrate the interplay between discrimination, whether it's based on gender, race, age, class, sexual identity, religion, or more." [2]

The agency of a person's body and mind is theirs and theirs alone. I am proud to be Shirley Cavanaugh's grandson.

I am proud to be the grandson of a sex worker.

These new thoughts inevitably brought me to think of the book my mother and her siblings tried to write in 1996.[68] I knew how important it was to them to get it right and have a better understanding of their mother. I also knew that, in 1999, everything that they had collected was boxed away in stacked corners of forgotten basements.

Several of those boxes were still in my storage. While I knew these boxes contained research regarding Shirley's life, I was never fully aware of their specific contents.

Also, much of the contents of these boxes was my mother's handwritten, 75-page suicide note ... something I wasn't capable of revisiting too often.

Every few years or so I would open a box and rifle through its contents.

Occasionally I would call phone numbers from my mother's address book, trying to find any relatives that were still around. I purchased a charger for her 2002 Nokia cell phone and when I turned it back on, I learned I was the last person she ever called.

This wasn't an easy project to take on.

---

[68] I think at one point my mother suggested its title to be "Hallowed Be My Life" but that never really stuck.

But it was a necessary one.[69]

For most of my life, I understood four basic ideas regarding Shirley Cavanaugh. Unwaveringly, this list became a soundbite that maintained Shirley's position as a sensationalized headline long after the last newspaper article about her was published.

The four ideas about Shirley were:

- She was a prostitute
- She shot a cop
- She abandoned all of her children
- She died of a brain tumor

This anemic list was, basically, all I had and, with minimal unpacking, all I was able to tell people about her. And so I held it, I believed it. I believed the reductive, unquestioned statement, "My grandmother was a prostitute," without understanding really what that meant at all.

So I decided to understand it.

In June 2022 I chose, like my mother and her siblings before me, to sit down and dedicate my time to Shirley's story.

I never could have predicted just how much of an emotional and familially complex journey I was actually setting out on.

---

[69] If you are familiar with the book "House of Leaves" by Mark Z. Danielewski — it is easy to see how this was my "Zampano's box," how Johnny Truant's relationship to his mother Pelafina reflected my relationship with my mother and why this book needed to be, in part, written like that one. I am profoundly grateful for what that book, and the corresponding album "Haunted" by Poe, have done for me over the past 20 years. They have carried me through many heart broken nights as I grieved the loss of my mother.

First I went to the Allegheny County Courthouse Archives Department and requested every file with the name Shirley Cavanaugh/Garretson/Lauterbach connected to them.

This was surprisingly easy and immediately fulfilling. I walked in, told them her names, and they told me to come back in two days. When I did, they had a stack of files. All of her arrests. The horrible behavior analysis. Everything concerning her legal troubles from 1955-1957. Profound.

I turned, then, to digital archives. Specifically *Ancestry.com, MyHeritage.com, Truthfinder.com*, and *Newspapers.com* which made it quite clear, and quickly: Shirley's story was entirely impossible to understand until present day …

Part of my family's research in the '90s involved the microfilm archives of the Carnegie Library. Within a few weeks they were able to uncover roughly ten or so articles about Shirley. All of them were easy to spot; they were front-page sensations that featured photographs of Shirley with headlines like, "Cop Now Admits Woman Shot Him." So they had them printed and filed away for research. In the past two decades, however, access to information has changed drastically.

What would have taken my family years to accomplish in the '90s is nearly instantaneous for me in 2022; in 1997, they were able to find ten or so articles using microfilm.

In 2022, with *Newspapers.com* — I am able to search over 860,000,000 articles for the name "Shirley Cavanaugh" in under one second.

Narrowing that search to Pennsylvania newspapers provided 504 mentions of her name. Further narrowing the results to articles between 1928-1972, regional to Pittsburgh, provided 361 mentions of her name. Of those 361, 326 contained relevant information related to Shirley's life and legal troubles. The rest consisted of a few misprints, another Shirley Cavanaugh in a different state, reprinted articles, obituaries of family members, and so on.

I cropped them all, and filed them, along with her legal documents, in chronological order on my computer, and began to read. I began to build, I began to see her.

Of the legal documents I was immediately intrigued ...

I knew about the prostitution charges and the gunshot but I didn't know about the assault of Eugene Coon nor about the Lauterbach house burglary. Initially, I set both aside as unconnected to what I was working on and continued to search for mentions of Carnahan, the gunshot, or The ABA.

Much to my surprise, I could find only one, vaguely-worded description of what had happened.

On page three of a six-page opinion piece written by Judge Montgomery in 1957:

> "... thereafter, she did report regularly to the Probation Office and would probably have reached the end of the three-year probation period uneventfully except for the *incident at the Sixth Avenue Club, which occurred on February 24, 1957 ...*" [3]

That was it.

At first I thought I must have missed something. I called the records department back.

They assured me they'd found everything there was to find.

I asked if they thought this was odd ...

I could hear them shrug through the phone.

It was obvious to me right then: I knew far less than I thought I did.

I turned to *Newspapers.com* and began to read ...

The first article was about her run-in with Eugene Coon in February of 1955. I matched this up with her 1955 legal documents and found Carnahan's signature on some of the intake forms. Thus establishing when they first met and broadening the scope of this story.

So I went back to Coon and the burglary and realized the entire timeline was relevant to the gunshot.

Later, when I found the *Pittsburgh Sun-Telegraph* article "Shirley Mum at Cop Trial: Carnahan Denies 'Affair'," I read how Carnahan explained meeting her and realizing he could use her as a "stool pigeon."

Shirley Cavanaugh court records

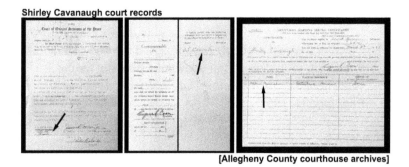

[Allegheny County courthouse archives]

Shirley Cavanaugh court records

That's when I started to really listen to what my grandmother was saying and not what other people were saying *about* her ...

The next article I came to was two years later: The Carnahan Affair.

As I read further, a story began to unfold that I had never considered. With everything laid out before me, I called my sister and father and told them about what I was learning. Both were as shocked as I was.

My grandmother was not just some prostitute who shot a cop. She was a sex worker who was tricked by one cop and manipulated by another. The gunshot was Carnahan's fault — not hers.

She turned to sex work to keep my infant mother ... alive.

Later, it became clear that each of the four ideas I had about Shirley were only partially true.

Her relationship to her children was far more complicated and nuanced than heartless abandonment. And she didn't have a brain tumor.

233

With each discovery, my heart would sink. My tears would flow. I would weep in my office.

Each time I found something astounding, I would post it to my Instagram and Facebook accounts and share the story gradually with my friends and family.[70]

But each time I would share these findings, a rock would be placed in my stomach, and I felt despair at the sole fact that I could never share any of this with my mom.

I could never show her that her adoption was fast-tracked while Shirley was being manipulated by the Pittsburgh Police. I could never tell Aunt Judy about the abandonment and abuses of Shirley's early life, and how that contributed to why Shirley treated Judy, Walter, and the Lauterbachs the way she did. I could never tell Uncle Jim about how his work contributed so profoundly to the creation of this book.

One of the last articles about Shirley was published on October 22nd, 1958. A photograph of her, blonde, with cigarette in hand on the front page of the *Pittsburgh Sun-Telegraph* with the headline, "Glad That's Over, Shirley Sighs." [71]

But it wasn't over for me.

Once I had made it to this point, I had nowhere else to go, the information I could easily find regarding Shirley was over.

I filed every article chronologically alongside every court document I had. I saw before me the story, the cover up, and Shirley's mistreatment at the hands of the Pittsburgh justice system.

---

[70] #FromTheFurnaceWithLove

[71] The final article written by Marilyn Ferguson.

At that point I had no choice; I had to confront the boxes that were in my basement.

I brushed off the dust, pulled back their lids, and cautiously laid out the files, photos, and papers before me and began to take inventory.

What I found was astonishing and unexpected: Aunt Judy's handwritten testimonials, my mother's collection of photographs, and Uncle Jim's work uncovering Shirley's history in Cleveland, Ohio. Furthermore, there were two separate timelines. One written by Judy and one by my father, Bruce. Each provided multiple narratives that would go on to help me corroborate the facts in this book.

But what did I have?

What did any of this mean if I couldn't share it with the people who helped create it?

What meaning do untied knots have when the hearts that held their tension are far gone?

I knew Mom had died. It's been 20 years. But I had no information regarding Judy or Jim.

So I dedicated myself to finding them.

It didn't matter if all I found of them were headstones — I would find them. So I scoured the boxes for anything that pointed in the direction of either of them.

One of the files I'd found was a list of phone numbers and addresses. A directory of Kirins, Horenskys, Cavanaughs, and Halls. I had thought I hit the jackpot, until after having called every number I found each of them had long since been disconnected.

Including all the numbers associated with Judy and Jim.

So I turned to the internet.

With the addresses and phone numbers I had associated with Jim, I was able to uncover two phone numbers for a Jim Garretson in Florida. And even though I had two of her previous addresses, I was unable to uncover any phone number for a Judy Lauterbach anywhere.

I called both of the numbers I found for Jim Garretson and left the following message:

> "My name is Jason, my mother's name was Ruth. If that doesn't mean anything to you — I have the wrong number and you can ignore this message.
>
> If those names do mean something to you …
>
> I have learned a lot about Shirley that I don't think we could have learned before. I've uncovered her court

documents, I've found every newspaper article. All of it. I'm writing this book, finally.

I don't know if this is you or even if you want to talk about this anymore. I know it's been 20 years.

But if it is you and you do want to talk more about this — please give me a call or send a text."

I left my phone number and I moved on to finding Judy.

What little I knew about her life were abstractions, ideas about who she may have been and where life may have taken her, but nothing concrete.

In the late '90s, Judy had made a few photo collages that she photocopied and mailed to Mom. The collages included pictures of her house, her address, her dog with a speech bubble saying "Hi Aunt Ruth," pot plants, and her joyfully smiling face. It was obvious she was excited to share all of this information with her sister.

Some of the photos had other people in them with their names written underneath.

With each photo, I pulled out details and tracked them down.

All of them were dead ends.

As to where Judy was, or even if she was still alive was an absolute mystery to me.

Nothing on *Ancestry.com* led me to her, nor could I find phone numbers or current addresses associated with her. Even with the old addresses I had for her, I found nothing.

So I turned to Facebook.

I searched the name Lauterbach and sent an identical message to roughly 50 people:

Hello!

I am messaging anyone in Pittsburgh with the last name Lauterbach in search of information on a few deceased relatives. Please feel free to ignore/discard this message if you find this does not apply to you.

My grandmother's name was Shirley Garretson, before that it was Shirley Lauterbach, before that, Shirley Cavanaugh.

Shirley married Walter Lauterbach in 1950. Together they had a daughter in 1951 or 1952 named Judy. She was my aunt.

I am writing a book about my mother Ruth and grandmother Shirley. However I, sadly, lack information regarding Judy, Walt and the Lauterbachs in general.

If you have any leads please let me know.

Otherwise, thank you for your time.

And this is how I met … Stephen Lauterbach, Judy's younger stepbrother.

"Judy was my stepsister," Stephen stated in a Facebook message.

My eyes filled with tears, in disbelief my breath was taken from me ...

> "Judy lived with us in Turtle Creek and then went to live with my grandparents in Wilkinsburg through High School. Both my sister and I went to visit her when she lived in Portland, Oregon. I was about 13 or 14 at the time. After my father passed we never heard from her again ... that was 2002 so — the last eight years of her life."

The last eight years of her life ...

My heart.

For Stephen, Judy died over a decade ago. For me — it was at that moment.

Judy died on June 28th, 2010.

Excessive alcohol and drug use had made her body incapable of recovering from a progressively worsening case of the autoimmune disease scleroderma.

Judy would never know the full story of her mother's life, and I would never have a chance to see my aunt again.

After Stephen and I exchanged a few messages, it became clear: the subjects of Shirley and Judy were not subjects the Lauterbachs wished would resurface.

I assured him of my intentions:

"I will never push. I will never ask any Lauterbach to bring anything up from the past they don't wish to discuss.

In the book I will talk about my connection to my Aunt Judy, the burglary and Shirley being married to Walt only as a matter of it happening.

I assure you my bias is only trying to make something our families will be proud of.

Something healing, something therapeutic, something that people will care about. Something that doesn't deprecate and belittle our families but rather elevates them and nurtures their stories."

After a few more exchanges it was obvious: Stephen and I had shared experiences that transcended the boundaries of relationships anchored to any specific person or decade. We both care about Judy, we both care about the Lauterbachs.

So we decided to meet.

Stephen came into Lawrenceville one afternoon and we had lunch at Industry Public House.

Both of us arrived with gifts.

I had photocopied the original court documents regarding the burglary and put them into a binder along with high quality printouts of every photo and collage I had of Aunt Judy. Many of which were of Mom and Judy at my parents' wedding, and a few of them were of Judy, Mom, and Uncle Jim in 1996, from when they first met.

Stephen brought me several photos of Judy from when she was a child. With his expressed permission I was able to use these photos to accentuate her section of this book.

Stephen also brought me two paintings done by one of Judy's boyfriends in the 1970s. One of the paintings is a kind of house/barn in a windstorm. The other is of a single mushroom growing amidst a similarly wind strewn, micro, landscape.[72]

When I showed Stephen the collages Aunt Judy sent my mother, he smiled, gave a chuckle. He recognized some of the people and places in the photos. Some of the photos were from when Judy's half-sister visited her in Oregon. I was elated to have these gaps filled in for me.

But then, despondently, Stephen paused.

---

[72] Another extremely beautiful coincidence: the lessons provided by psychedelic mushrooms are an important aspect of my life. These paintings were done in the '70s, Stephen kept them because his father, Walter, loved them. He gave them to me and said, "perhaps you can find some new meaning in them." After abstaining from psychedelics for well over two years, Stephen gave me this painting the day after my most recent psychedelic journey. I felt this was a hint from Judy, telling me how correct of a path I was on.

"Do you remember 'The Cop and the Call Girl'?" he asked.

Assuring him that I did, he followed with, "That article was devastating to my father and our entire family ..."

Walter Lauterbach belonged to The Silent Generation and always remained that way. He never spoke too in-depth about his relationship with Shirley and by 1996, Walter had long since been remarried with children. Away from his past, 40 years later, Walter's ex-wife was back in the news. And while the last name Lauterbach was never used in that article, Walter's family knew the name Shirley Cavanaugh.

"That period of his life was something he tried not to relive,"[73] Stephen explained. "It was hard watching my father explain some of the things that were coming out in the paper."

Stephen would go on to tell me more about Walter than I had ever heard before. Walter was in the Navy and served in both WW2 and the Korean War. He was a clarinet player in the Naval band. A taxi-driver. He was a kind man. A loving man. A good father and someone Stephen holds in great reverence. When I go onto Stephen's Facebook page and look at photos of Walter in his old age, holding a beer, wearing a sweatshirt that reads, "World's greatest grandpa," I can see a softness in his eyes. I see a man who struggled. I see a man who cared. Walter, like my father, like Shirley, like my mother — he, too, did his best at being who he was.

After all Stephen told me, it's apparent that Walter was able to rebuild his life and find solace after his time with Shirley.

---

[73] Judy's writing reflects a moment of this understanding too: "My mother once said in a newspaper quote that her time with my father was the most peaceful of her life. I believed that. Just as I believed that his time with her was the least peaceful of his life."

While there is no actual relationship between us, I like to think of Stephen as an honorary uncle. He spent much more time with my Aunt Judy than I was ever able to. With the gifts he gave me, the paintings, the photos, the stories, I was able to piece together Judy's section of this book in a way that would not have been possible before we met. Sometimes we still text each other, he's a good person. He's also funny as all get-out. I will be forever grateful for his contributions to this book.

The loss of Judy stayed with me for quite a while after that meeting. The impact was also noticeable on my sister Megan.

However brief it may have been, Judy and Megan shared a connection.

Perhaps something in the hearts of the strong line of Cavanaugh women beats in ways invisible to the rest of us.

Now what?

Judy was dead, Mom was dead. Grandma Elsa, Pappap Art. Audrey and Bob.

Shirley.

Everyone was dead and gone.

But I kept my promise, I finished what they started.

But what was all of this worth?

I untied the knots.

But did it matter?

It did.

On the morning of December 19th, 2022, I woke up to a new voicemail and message on my phone waiting for me …

> "Jason, I left a message.
>
> Yes, I'm the guy you're looking for.
>
> Would love to talk to you.
>
> Call me."

"My god!" I gasped and grabbed my wife's hand. "It's Uncle Jim!"

I didn't hesitate. I called as quickly as I could.

"Hello! Hi! Uncle Jim!" I stammered (it had been 20 years).

"Jason, how've you been? What's up?" Jim replied.

"I've learned a lot about Shirley," I said. "I don't think we could have learned this before the digital age. I ..." I paused. "I'm sorry. It's been so long. Do you want to talk about this? Is this all the past for you?"

I could hear a lighter spark up a joint as he inhaled smoothly, exhaling, sitting outdoors on a hot Florida night as he said, "Jason ... tell me everything."

I filled my lungs and just let go.

"I decided to finish the book about Shirley ..."

I told him about *Newspapers.com* and *Ancestry.com*. About the courthouse documents and the interviews. I told him about the photos I purchased and about the orphanage records. I told him about Stephen. I told him about my life, my wife, my sister, and my father.

I spent an hour talking and by the end was entirely out of breath.

"I am going to finish this book," I told him. "I can't believe I found you. I had planned on putting a note in the book with my contact information in case you ever found it and read it."

Uncle Jim was not only still interested in this story, but became immediately invested in my progress from that moment forward.

I set up a Google drive folder with everything I had found and sent him the links. Asked him to take some days and read over what I found and we could get back to talking.

"In the meantime," Jim told me, "you're going to have to give me your address. I've got a lot to send you. Apparently, I was holding onto everything waiting for this day to come."

Over the next few weeks Uncle Jim would text me in astonishment,

> "I'm reading these Marilyn Ferguson interviews ... This is the first time I've read my mother's voice ... Jason ... One of these documents has her Social Security Number on it ... I've been searching for that for years ..."

Then — the packages started to arrive. From the contents of these packages I was able to fill in the necessary information to construct the very pages of this book. Some of the contents of which were:

> ➤ Shirley's Ouija Board from the 1960s
> ➤ A set of Shirley and John's silverware
> ➤ A lock of Shirley's hair in an envelope. On the outside of the envelope, an easily recognizable handwriting: Grandma Elsa had written, while Parkinson's shook her hand, "Shirley Garretson died Nov 7th, 1972"[74]
> ➤ John Garretson's personal photo albums of his time with Shirley and Forrest
> ➤ All of Forrest's belongings, including a clay disk with his handprint on the front and his name scratched into the back, drawings from his first-grade classmates and his first-grade vocabulary work books,[75] and Forrest's obituary, autopsy, and all of his medical records
> ➤ There were also pictures of Forrest — in his casket
> ➤ Copies of all of Mom's files
> ➤ Copies of both Dad's and Judy's timelines

---

[74] See page 156.

[75] All of which were, tragically, only half finished.

- Original newspapers
- A coat of arms for the Cavanaugh name
- Shirley's vintage gold toned, Art Deco, Zaima brand Celeste Lighter from the 1950s

Occasionally Uncle Jim still finds things in storage and, when he has a boxful, he sends them my way. I catalog and file them accordingly. With every photograph and document he sends me, I scan them, label them appropriately, and then put them into a Google Drive folder we both share. In some cases, such as many old medical forms, I transcribed the text that was too difficult to read.

I would also send the medical files to a family friend, and nurse practitioner, Ash Kehoe, who would interpret the doctors notes for me. I would add her paraphrases to the back of the transcribed files.

Uncle Jim's packages allowed me to knit together everything that I had. With John's photographs, and Forrest's belongings, I was able to piece together Shirley's life after The Carnahan Affair. I look forward to visiting him someday soon in Florida and catching up with him in person. Until then, as well as after, we plan on remaining in each other's lives. Sometimes I text him and let him know how thankful I am for all of his work, and how proud I am for all he accomplished. He responds in kind.

After seeing the cover of this book for the first time Uncle Jim texted me and said, "I don't know if you know this, but the first time your mother saw that picture she said these exact words: 'That needs to be the cover of the book if we write one.'"[76]

Sometimes we get high on the other end of each other's phone and, like Mom and me drunk in a church parking lot, we laugh

---

[76] As far as I remember the photo I used for the cover was an accident, a malfunction of our home printer in 1996.

and talk for hours into the night. He's a good human. To be able to reconnect with him has been a profound experience.

When he reminds me how proud and supportive he is of the work I am doing — in his voice, I can hear Shirley, I can hear Aunt Judy, and I can hear Mom.

And in those moments — I can smell the flowers my mother told me to remember.

Here, at the end of this book, I hope you, reader, can smell them too.

Shirley's Zaima Celeste lighter

Cavanaugh coat of arms

[Garretson personal collection]

[Garretson personal collection]

Shirley's Ouija Board

Forrest Garretson handprint age: four

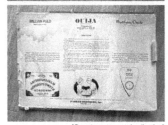

[Garretson personal collection]

[Garretson personal collection]

[1] Miano, Audrey "Feminism 101: What Is A SWERF?" *FEM*, 15 July 2017, https://femmagazine.com/feminism-101-what-is-a-swerf/

[2] International Women's Development Agency. "What Does Intersectional Feminism Actually Mean?" IWDA, 13 Aug. 2023, iwda.org.au/what-does-intersectional-feminism-actually-mean.

[2] Montgomery, J. Commonwealth of Pennsylvania vs. Shirley Cavanaugh, NO. 42 March Sessions 1954 In Burglary. OPINION and ORDER OF THE COURT. Date of Information March 11, 1957. *Allegheny County Records Dept.*

"Now that I'm here, I hear you
And wonder if maybe you can hear yourself
Ringing in me now that you're somewhere else
'Cause I hear your strange music, gentle and true
Singing inside me with the best parts of you ..."

Poe, from "If You Were Here"

The Past Isn't What It Used to Be

When I look into the deep past of the 1920s and find myself here in the present moments of the early-2020s, a strange refraction occurs. This book has become a lens through which my perspective changes. A lens through which I may view my mother and my grandmother more effectively. More respectfully. More specifically ... through the lens of intersectionality.

A perspective that wasn't possible during Shirley's life and not really well known during my mom's life.[77] Shirley was not some destitute prostitute abandoning children and causing trouble for the police. Shirley was born into poverty, during the Depression, in a polluted suburb, repeatedly abandoned, abused, manipulated. A mother with no helpful resources. Mentally ill. Alcoholic.

My mother's intersections ring similarly.

Both of their stories deserved a holistic understanding. Both of these women deserve more respect than society was ever able to give either of them.

Aunt Judy, Uncle Jim, and Mom were all, within weeks of their births, abandoned by Shirley.

Within the first year of my life my mother, too, had to take ample space from us. When I ask, "Why?" a complete answer still eludes me. Perhaps, simply, some traumatized people traumatize people. I don't believe this as any kind of axiom speaking hyperbolically. No traumatized person is a monolith. Shirley was abandoned, abused, manipulated, and traumatized by nearly everyone in her life. And so much of it was spilled across the front-page news.

---

[77] Kimberlé Crenshaw didn't introduce the concept into modern vernacular until the late 1980s.

Accordingly, she behaved in ways befitting of someone with her experiences, I am not the least bit shocked when I notice her patterns in her children.

Both experience and research have taught me that the lifelong impact of early childhood traumas is this: if our amygdala response is activated repeatedly at an age where neither fight nor flight is an option, then our foundation, the basic framework upon which we grow, is faulty. [1]

These early experiences will therefore influence our mental, emotional, and physical growth indefinitely. So early childhood trauma, even forgotten trauma, remains.

Furthermore, trauma is not isolated to the moment of the incident. If there are external, or internal, stimuli that trigger a visceral response to the memory of that trauma, the body has a real, relived response to the original trauma. Trauma is not just the incident but also every moment afterwards. Each moment that led to the present moment.

Trauma is constant.

Hence I imprint fears of abandonment onto current relationships regardless of them being neither my past relationships nor my parents. I do this because the sensation of the closeness of love triggers, firstly and unfortunately, the closeness of trauma. The closeness of distance. Of loss.[78]

---

[78] At times, by both of my parents, I have felt abandoned, at times I felt abused. But the details of my traumas, I feel, serve little to no purpose by being in this book. That's what my therapist and my support network are for.

I know … I'm no doctor. But I do understand Hebb's Law.[79] I understand thoughts that fire together, wire together. And when we live in a system of perpetual feedback between trauma triggers and simply living, we live in a system where wounds left by our traumas barely have room to breathe … Let alone heal.

Making the maneuverability of basic reality … complicated as fuck.

It certainly did for Shirley and my mother. And it certainly has for me.[80] I'm sure, at times, it has also for my sister Megan.

[Personal collection]

That being said, our relationship as siblings has been wonderful. We were close in childhood and have remained close into adulthood. We are both very supportive of the other and put care into our relationship. At least monthly we get wine-drunk over Zoom and laugh chatting until late into the night.

We've both had our relationships. Our ups and downs. Depression. Anxiety. We both experience panic attacks. We both still experience the adversity of our childhoods through triggers and unconscious reinforcing.

---

[79] "… if a cell persistently activates another nearby cell, the connection between the two cells becomes stronger …" [2]

[80] I'm sure, at times, it has also for you, reader.

254

But like our mother and grandmother before us — this is not the extent of who we are.

My sister Megan will never fully comprehend the extent of the love and admiration I have for her and her life choices. She is strong, confident, empathetic, and vulnerable. And I will look to her for light and guidance for as long as I live.

When I look at her lineage, I am overwhelmingly impressed by the women that led to her. From Alma, to Shirley, to Mom, to Megan. And all of that complemented by the overwhelming love of Elsa Horensky.

Elsa Horensky, Jason Kirin, Megan Kirin

She is strength and support — embodied. I admire and love her deeply.

Over one of our Zoom dates I asked her, "Alma … Shirley … Judy … Mom … You … How does it feel to be the last in the long line of Cavanaugh women? How does it feel to have that history as yours?"

At which point we both just sighed. Made some guttural noises. Looked down and around hoping some answer would come to either of us. But all she could say was, "Fuck, I don't even know."

Our lives, our genes, our generational trauma, is what drives us both to become the best versions of ourselves. Our adversity is our greatest teacher, our greatest motivator. The best parts of the Cavanaughs, the Horenskys, and the Kirins are what make us who we are.

Megan has become a great adventurer over the years and she consistently astounds me with her journeys across life and love.

Once she biked and hiked the Appalachian Trail. The trail that John Garretson walked all these years ago.

On her travels she came across the Appalachian Trail Conservancy Visitor's Center. When she went inside there was a long book shelf holding decades of Polaroid photo albums. Each of them were filled with photographs of the individuals who visited there over the years.

Remembering the stories John Garretson had told us when we met him in 1996, Megan began flipping through the pages of these albums until, amazingly, she found a Polaroid labeled "John H. Garretson (Just John), Cape Coral Flr."

So she took a photo of her own.

Excellent.

What I feel this book has done for us both is provide us with a telescope into our past, a lens through which we can see the stories of our grandmother and mother more clearly. This book has given us a way to look back on everything that happened and say, "I, too, am trying my best, I love you. I forgive you. I forgive me."

Furthermore, like Walter and John after Shirley, our father was able to rebuild his life and find fulfillment. Our relationship is also a point of pride for me, rarely, in nearly two decades, have we ever missed meeting up for coffee every Sunday morning. There came a point where I think we really figured our shit out.

What's more, he has long since been remarried to a woman who truly fulfills him, a woman we are proud to have as a stepmother. Together they've retired and spend most of their time rehabilitating bunny rabbits so that they may be adopted.

In their home, there are always a minimum of three bunnies. It is adorable and makes visiting their home always a treat.

But what does it all matter? What does all of this account for? Where is the light in all of this? At first I thought this book was just a means by which I could better comprehend and connect with Shirley's story. To see Shirley Cavanaugh as more than just exaggerated familial mythos. To learn something about genetics. To expend an exercise into healing generational trauma. To visit the places where Shirley lived and breathe in the air left there. To be able to ponder whether Shirley and I would have been able to relate to each other as grandson and grandmother.

I think we would have.

But it's only now, late editing on August 20th, 2023, that I see the truth.

I thought I was telling the story of Shirley and, subsequently, how her kids dedicated themselves to collaboration.

I thought I was telling a story about them.

But ... I am them.

This book ... is about *my* mother.

It is about me facing my grief and in turn ... letting it go.

By seeing her life's intersectionality. And seeing her through stories she would have wanted to be told about her. By listening to memories of the years she spent flabbergasted to be alive and dancing. I see who my mom really was.

I see her, I hear her for the first time.

And I can feel my resentments fail.

The parts of me that grew hardened have sloughed off into feather beds.

I will always love her. I will always miss her.

Only now, I feel the weight of her presence in my heart to be lighter than ever before.

She is the core of it all. The ultimate dovetail conjoining my space and time.

Mom's abandonment and early childhood adversity lived within her body and guided her reality through shadowed pain. Her heart grasped at invisible reins to steer her clear from ever facing again the dangers she faced at her most vulnerable points.

And it worked — until it didn't.

It isn't lost on me that, sometimes, my words echo hers, and that her words echoed Shirley's.

It's trauma all the way down.

My parents and their parents and theirs too, each acted in accord with only what they understood. Culture was a factor. Religion was a factor. Society, education, economics. All of it.

And at this chaotic intersection they were always, all ways, trying their best.

Their family is my family. Audrey, Shirley's sister, I knew as my aunt my whole life. I was close to both her and her husband Bob. They were also Megan's godparents. Janet, Shirley's niece, my first cousin once removed, I knew and loved as an aunt my entire life. Jim and Judy will always be my uncle and my aunt, they will always live within my heart and the genes we share.

And as I am their genes — I am them, I am all of us, reaching through time and from beyond the distance of death, compiling this book. Telling a story of the names Cavanaugh, Lauterbach, Horensky, and Kirin so that we may look back upon them with love, vulnerability, empathy, and courage.

Things have changed. We are different here. Without resentments. Bearing the lightness of forgiveness and calm detachment.

And I couldn't have done it without my family.

All of them.

As this book closes now, somehow, I open.

[1] Harris, Nadine Burke. "How childhood trauma affects health across a lifetime." *TEDMED* Feb. 2015.
https://www.tedmed.com/talks/show?id=293066

[2] https://thedecisionlab.com/thinkers/neuroscience/donald-hebb

From Bullet to Box Step

Here we are, at the end of a story that took nearly a century to unfold and three decades to put into sustainable words.

I know these are the last few sentiments I am going to be writing about Shirley and my mom; I can see them clearly now.

But there is one last story I want to tell ...

And I saved it until the end on purpose ...

The etymology of *coincidence*: to fall upon a moment, together.

But that doesn't say enough for this final, fallen set of shared moments ...

In 1996 when Uncle Jim, Aunt Judy, and Mom were beginning their research, a detail stood out to my dad.

A detail that stole the oxygen from the room ...

"I couldn't believe it," Dad told me. "136 6th St. It couldn't have been, there was no way."

A coincidence so *perfectly* unique, it is hard to fully grasp ...

"I remember the day your mother and I were doing research on Shirley when I noticed it."

My father recalls, "Shirley, Ruth's mother, shot this cop Carnahan at The ABA downtown at 136 6th St., right?"

He grunts.

"Now this was the 1990s, so we didn't have iPhones. We couldn't just *Google* the address, but we knew it, '136 6th St.' We

261

knew we knew it. So, we all got in the car and drove Downtown. We parked and walked to 6th St."

I can hear his shoulders drop over the phone, I know his voice, deepening, he says, "I looked at your mom, her mouth is just gaping, she's breathless, she says, you must be kidding me ..."

He breathes in ...

"It was Arthur Murray's ... The dance studio where your mom was a teacher, where we met."

[Personal collection]

"We went inside ... There was still a bar where people could sit and chat in the room ... I don't know if it was the same bar, but ... in 1979 we met there ...

We met *in the room* where the shot was fired — 22 years after the gun went off ..."

My parents met because, coincidentally, my mother danced and my father was brave.

They met and they danced across the floors where Shirley defended herself two decades earlier.

They danced across the floors where Carnahan collapsed and where Rosenberg called witness after witness ... and neither of them knew anything about it.

They only knew — they were there to dance.

To be brave and to move.

I've carried this story with me since then. I'm not certain what it means.

Sometimes I think it is so astronomically unique just so that I would always carry it with me.

So that I would listen. So that I would believe in Shirley.

So that I would never forget how important this story was to tell.

Where to Donate in Shirley Cavanaugh's Name

Intersectional feminism is the only ideology capable of carrying humanity into any kind of future worth living in.[81]

Unless we consider the entire story and stop making synecdoches of individual moments in a person's life, we fail her. We fail him. We fail them.

That being said ...

Where there is acceptance, progress, and intersectionality, there are those who wish to oppose these values.

But let's be clear.

Any exclusionary principle is <u>counter</u> to feminism.

Sex-Worker Exclusionary Radical Feminists (SWERFS) are <u>not</u> feminists in any way.

They're just assholes.

Stories are complicated. Life is complex.

To understand people fully, to be empathetic, to make sure there is justice — we must consider *all* the intersections a person faces in this system.

If you or someone you know has the time and energy to put into SWERF ideology, I advise you to read this book again.

There are stories you will never know, as complicated as yours, with factors far out of anyone's control.

---

[81] To learn about intersectional feminism, read the works of Kimberlé Crenshaw.

Now take that energy and redirect it constructively.

Get your wallet out, take out your Venmo or Cashapp, and donate to the Pittsburgh chapter of The Sex Worker Outreach Program (SWOP) ...

"Sex Workers Outreach Project (SWOP) is a social justice network focusing on ending the violence and stigma associated with sex work through education and advocacy. SWOP PGH connects sex workers to social services, works with local health institutions, and most recently organized a mutual aid fund to support sex workers impacted by the pandemic." [1]

If Shirley had SWOP instead of manipulative police, perhaps her story would have turned out differently. Perhaps she would have become an archeologist, or would have been able to go to business school. Perhaps she and my mother would have had more of a chance to develop their early relationship. Perhaps not.

I just know that empathy and nurturance is in short supply these days.

Visit their main page at https://swoppittsburgh.com/ to learn more about SWOP and visit their donation page at https://swoppittsburgh.com/donate to access their Venmo and their CashApp.

It would truly move me for those donations to be made in her honor. To leave her legacy as one of charity, care, support, inclusivity. When you drop that donation make sure to sign it...

"Friends of Shirley."

Sex Workers Outreach Project, Pittsburgh Chapter
- https://swoppittsburgh.com/donate

[1] https://swoppittsburgh.com/

Acknowledgments

Amanda Blair: When I began this project I knew that I was embarking on an emotionally complicated journey. While I had a therapist to talk to throughout ... I needed you, someone who cares, intimately. The history of my family, the experiences my mother and grandmother suffered, the experiences I had as a child, all of this has made my life's maneuverability, to say the least, complicated. I have deep depressive episodes, panic attacks, sometimes I cannot see the way out. Sometimes I think the whole thing is just going to consume everything I am.

Sometimes I'm afraid the whole world is going to abandon me.

And then I see you. I feel your fingers in my hair as I cry. I feel how much you care about my story, my mother, my family.

How strong you are to come home daily to find me often crying, writing, broken hearted over family trauma, only to reach out your hand and guide me to a safe, soft, space where I could cry and talk about what I was learning.

Sometimes when we were out with friends and someone would ask me how the book was going I would only get a few sentences in before you perked up and began talking about the project too. I'd sit back and watch as you spout off detail after detail, story after story. You listened. I saw how much this story meant to you too. You took care of it. You took care of me. You held me through this. You guided me back to safety when it became too difficult.

For most of my life I never could have dreamed of meeting someone I could marry and share my life with. How could that even be remotely possible with my past? With my family history?

But you know every detail. You know all of it and still you look me in the eye with joy. You look at me with love. With support. With empathy. With a shared understanding that life is a complex fucking mess.

Against so many psychological odds.

Here we are.

Thank you, genuinely, for your delicacy, your care. My stability would have been far more shaky without your support.

As deep as history, I love you.

Dana Kaufman, Satellite, Editor:

There was no other person who could have done for this book what Dana did. The dedication, compassion, and care they put forth in editing this book was profoundly moving.

We worked alongside each other in a Google Docs file called "Outline" and every day I would open the file and see the entire formatted structure shifted a few inches to the left. Indicating that a slew of new comments had been added to the right side margins.

Sometimes the comments would be explaining the differences between en and em dashes. Sometimes they would stress that I clean up my tense shifts or that I need to decide, and stick with, either using the Oxford comma or not. Dana's attention to formatting and grammar was unmatched. Their attention to the detailed intricacies of form I have never experienced before.

But it was Dana's empathy and personal understanding that truly provided them with the path upon which they were capable of caring not only for the form but for the content as well.

Dana understood this story. Dana cared about this story. Sometimes I would find comments from them that were a paragraph or two long explaining medical aspects of childbirth, or

269

feminist ideology, or ways in which they felt they connected to my maternal lineage. Sometimes I would find subtle, yet effective, criticisms about unintentional ableist language or when my perspective was too much through the male gaze. Dana also understood that, in the main narration, I didn't want to tell this story in first-person narration until the year I was actually born. I felt that the "egoic I" narrator didn't belong in Shirley's story. There were multiple times where my language reflected a "fourth wall break" far too soon and Dana caught and corrected them.

Furthermore our deadline was met. Without fail, without hesitation or delay.

They have been attentive, supportive, and fully dedicated to this project from day one.

This book would be an absolute mess without them.

Calling the book a "Tapestry" was their idea … and they were instrumental in weaving it together.

John Vargas: It is amazing and wonderful to me that John and I have remained in such close touch because of this book. Growing up, I was always aware that John was the man in my mother's life before my father. She had a photo album of them dancing. When she shared memories of him, she was always smiling. When I asked what happened to him she'd always say, "Moved out to Hollywood, became an actor, we lost touch." Every once in a while I would peruse an album of mom's photos that had pictures of her and John. I'd always end up visiting his IMDB page[82] and get a kick out of him being from Mom's life. But because of this book, I actually signed up for IMDB and emailed his agent. Subject: "ISO: John Vargas, writing a book about my mother in the 1970s. They danced together..." Etc. I attached some photos to the email but didn't really expect anything to come of it. John called me the next morning — ecstatic. He couldn't wait to share stories about dancing with Mom. We still text each other random thoughts about disco and Mom. He's put together a few playlists for me to listen to. He tells me they are all songs that Mom loved to dance to. It's an absolute treasure to listen to these songs and picture her dancing to them. I am certain John and I will remain in touch as time moves on. The way he talks about Mom is beautiful, he loved her in a time before children. Before the suburbs. Before everything changed. Sometimes I send John songs I've grown to love over the years, often he tells me that through these songs he can see that Mom is still in touch with me. What an unexpected friendship to develop in my life at the age of 41.

---

[82] https://www.imdb.com/name/nm0889855/

[Personal collection]

Uncle Jim: What could I possibly say that would make due? How can I talk about Uncle Jim in such a way that it won't fall short? Jim is the reason this whole thing exists. Had it not been for him, would we have ever found John Garretson? Forrest's grave? Shirley's hospital records in Cleveland? I don't know.

What I do know is I am grateful to have my uncle back in my life. This whole book is a testament to the strength and perseverance of my mother's family and he is one of the last of them. When I talk to him, I talk to mom. I talk to Judy. I talk to Shirley. I will cherish our relationship for the rest of my days.

I will forever be grateful and astonished by the effort he put into uncovering the materials that have allowed me to create this book.

Mackenzie Carpenter: The investigative journalist who wrote the article, "The Cop and the Call Girl, The Legacy of a Pittsburgh Shooting: A Family Pulls Itself Together." To say her work was indispensable or incomparable falls short. She wrote an archive of us, one that both Uncle Jim and myself visit often. When Jim and I talk about it, I can hear his voice - this was a monument to his efforts. This was his goal. This article was his trophy, his proud accomplishment.

I managed to catch up with Mackenzie Carpenter a few months ago. Unfortunately, she told me, her memory isn't what it used to be and that she only remembers the article and the story vaguely.

But as it stands - her work on my family is the predecessor to this book. Her research built for our family a bridge into the past. A window into a specific period of our lives directly before everyone disbanded.

In a way, this book is the sequel to that article.

The greatest of my gratitudes and depthless admiration for her and her work. Sincerely, Mackenzie Carpenter, thank you for caring, thank you for helping our family accomplish what we did.

Brandon Keller and Lawrence Fisher: Two highly intelligent and knowledgeable lawyer friends of mine who I could text anytime I had questions about Shirley's legal troubles. I'd always get quick, reliable, and succinct answers.

Art and Elsa Horensky: I cannot stress enough how profoundly perfect these two were as my grandparents. I loved both of them deeply, truly. Their support and care was unmatched. Grandma Elsa and I would have weekly visits until a week before her death. She was marvelously empathetic and loved everyone. Often my friends would visit with me. The more far out punk or goth they were — the more Grandma loved them. I cherish the time I had with them with great love and gratitude.

Aunt Janet: Shirley's niece, technically my first cousin once removed. She is a dear member of my mother's family. I'm grateful to have connected with her as a result of this project. She tells me stories about mom and her like they grew up as sisters. It is endearing. She brings such warmth to my mother's early years.

Louis Rosenberg: I am forever grateful for this man's dedication to truth and to justice. Had it not been for him, I fear Shirley would have, likely, just been lost to the system. I could go on extensively about Rosenberg and my feelings for him; instead, I am sharing his obituary in which Bill Heltzel of the *Post-Gazette* pontificates Rosenberg's life and death poignantly.

By Bill Heltzel
Post-Gazette Staff Writer

Retired federal Judge Louis Rosenberg, resented by some lawyers for his unbending enforcement of courtroom rules but regarded by others as incorruptible and a model of propriety, died Friday.

Judge Rosenberg died of an undisclosed cause at his home in Highland Park. He would have been 101 tomorrow.

He was appointed to the federal bench in Pittsburgh in 1961 and served to around 1991. Previously, he was public safety director in Pittsburgh.

Judge Rosenberg was known as a no-nonsense jurist. Men were expected to wear jackets, and he kept extras in a closet in case a witness showed up dressed inappropriately.

Lawyers who thanked him for a ruling were harshly reprimanded.

"That was one of his idiosyncrasies," said Joseph Weis, senior judge in the U.S. District Court of Appeals. "He was not doing you a favor. He was simply doing his duty and it was not proper to thank him for doing his duty."

Many lawyers bristled under his courtroom demeanor. In 1976 and 1979, Allegheny County Bar Association surveys gave Judge Rosenberg failing grades. The latter poll rated him the lowest among 12 U.S. District Court jurists for impartiality, legal ability, diligence and temperament.

The late Post-Gazette columnist Joe Browne wrote after the 1979 survey that Judge Rosenberg was known as "Loony Lou." "He's the kind of person who always seems to be rubbing sandpaper on sunburned backs."

"I would dissent from any description of him as being loony," said U.S. District Court Chief Judge Donald E. Ziegler. "He was incorruptible and hard-working, and he had a real sense of propriety. He was difficult at times because he enforced the rules. Some of the criticism of him over the years by the bar was occasioned by the fact that lawyers were required to tow the line in his room like in no other room."

Another criticism was that he took too long to render decisions. In a high-profile patent infringement case involving Jones & Laughlin Steel Corp., he issued a 742-page decision two years after the courtroom phase ended in 1968. The 3rd U.S. Circuit Court of Appeals quickly rejected his ruling.

1961 photo

Louis Rosenberg

His legendary slowness was the result of good intentions. He labored over every decision, to make sure that he was correct and fair, said U.S. District Court Magistrate Judge Robert Mitchell, who served as his law clerk for several years.

"He was extremely conscientious," Weis said. "He desperately wanted to be right in his rulings, so he left no stone unturned and he debated with himself over and over again."

He imposed tough sentences. In 1969, he presided in USA vs. American Standard, an antitrust case against manufacturers of plumbing fixtures accused in a $1 billion price fixing scheme. The jury found the defendants guilty. Judge Rosenberg not only imposed fines on the companies, he sentenced corporate executives to jail.

Ziegler thinks Judge Rosenberg developed a law-and-order judicial philosophy from his days as public safety director. That philosophy sometimes put him out of synch with the more liberal philosophy of the Warren Court. As a result, Ziegler said, Judge Rosenberg was reversed on appeal "a fair amount of times."

"He was not substantially wrong," Ziegler said. "There was just a different philosophy that existed. ... I would rate him a very fair man."

Nathaniel Glosser, his grandson, said

Judge Rosenberg believed that his most important job as a federal judge was looking out for the rights of ordinary Americans. He thinks his grandfather inherited a strict sense of right and wrong, and respect for law, from his own parents, Eastern European Jewish immigrants who settled in Beaver Falls.

Judge Rosenberg was born on July 5, 1898 and was one of seven children. After his father died, he supported the family with a job as traveling salesman. He attended night school at Duquesne University and got his law degree in 1923.

The lifelong bachelor adopted and raised his sister's daughter.

He worked as solicitor for several school districts and local governments and became active in the Allegheny County Democratic Party. His connections led to several political appointments, for example, with the Home Owners Loan Corp. during the Depression and Allegheny County Emergency Relief.

He campaigned for Mayor David L. Lawrence, who named him director of public safety in 1956. He didn't believe in sitting behind a desk. When there was a fire after midnight, he was often there. He established a police K-9 unit. And he was known for testing police by calling in complaints under a fictitious name and then monitoring how long it took to respond.

"He talked about his years as director a great deal," Glosser said. "He had a lot of fun."

Lawrence persuaded President John F. Kennedy to appoint Judge Rosenberg to the federal bench. The nomination was controversial because Judge Rosenberg was already 62 and had not previously served as a judge.

In 1976 he became a senior judge. The change entitled him to a reduced schedule, but he continued to handle a full caseload.

After he retired, he worked on two books, a memoir and a novel. Neither has been published.

He is survived by his daughter, Marcia Swartz Glosser of Johnstown and grandsons Nathaniel Glosser of Lawrenceville and Gregory Glosser of Sunnyvale, Calif.

A funeral will be held Tuesday at Ralph Schugar Chapel, 5509 Centre Ave., Shadyside. Visitation will begin at 12:30 p.m. and the service will begin at 1:30 p.m. He will be buried in a private ceremony at B'Nai Israel Cemetery, Penn Hills.

John V. Snee: Another individual for whom I would have trouble paraphrasing my feelings. Without him, what would have happened to Shirley? Would anyone else have cared as much as he did? Was he just some public defender randomly assigned to Shirley's case?

I don't know.

I just know my gratitude for him is depthless.

Snee went on to retire to Florida, where he lived until the age of 88. He died from a heart attack.

But there was one other case Snee was on that moved me: in 1966, Snee represented a trans woman named Roberta.

He fought for Roberta's legal right to not only change her name, but also her biological sex. Snee even acquired and presented a letter to the courts from a surgeon as to why this surgery was necessary for Roberta so that she may begin to live life the way she was born to.

Nearly 60 years ago this man stood up for trans rights and nearly 70 years ago he stood up for the rights of a sex worker.

John V. Snee, you have my everlasting respect and admiration.

Thank you.

RICHARD WOULD BE ROBERTA

Father of 2 Plans to Change Sex

A 31-year-old Brentwood father of two petitioned Common Pleas Court yesterday for permission to change his name from Richard to Roberta because he hopes to change his sex.

The unusual request was filed by Richard C. Nelson, of 128 West Bellecrest Ave., a traveling salesman for a Pittsburgh firm.

If the court approves the petition, Nelson's name will be changed to Roberta Catherine Nelson.

According to the petition, doctors have advised Nelson to undergo hormonal and surgical corrections for "sex reassignment."

The petitioner declared the operations

and treatments will transform his sex to that of a female and said the change of name is necessary for social reasons.

Nelson is the father of two children —a boy and a girl—and was married until last July when his wife petitioned for and was granted a divorce on routine grounds.

His case was described by his attorney, John V. Snee, as "similar to the Christine Jorgensen case."

Miss Jorgensen was an ex-GI who was surgically transformed from male to female in 1952 and changed his her name from George to Christine.

Snee said Nelson now dresses and talks like a woman and is gradually

assuming many of the physical characteristics of a woman. He described his client as "an attractive woman" when he wears a wig.

The attorney said the operation would be performed in the United States when Nelson is able to finance it.

"He simply feels more like a woman than a man and believes he is doing what must be done," Snee said.

The attorney said Nelson's children are "nice kids" and are "as normal as applie pie."

Judge John P. Hester set a hearing on the proposed name change for Nov. 17 at 9:30 a. m.

Pittsburgh Post Gazette Tues. Oct. 18, 1966.

Marilyn Ferguson: In a sea of sensationalized news articles, Ferguson interviewed Shirley multiple times. As far as I could uncover, Ferguson wrote five articles concerning Shirley on a personal, emotional, and empathetic level. Without these interviews, we would never have heard Shirley's voice. Ferguson also seemed like an appropriate woman to have become close to Shirley, both of them making a name for themselves in the 1950s as strong women who cared. In my research of Ferguson, I came across this truly marvelous article of hers titled, "Learn jujitsu, girls, and you'll be safer." The article features several photos of Ferguson in a ball gown with elbow length gloves beating the ever living shit out of a man in a bomber jacket. Incredible. Truly an icon and hero to me. This book would not have been possible without her.

Mark B. Morrow: In my first book, "From Farmland to Card Shop: A History of Shadyside Through the Windows of 5522 Walnut St." I had to work with various local archivists uncovering non-modern photographs of Shadyside, Pennsylvania. I found a Facebook group called, "Friends of Shadyside," where I could post my findings and learn more about what I was looking at. Quickly the comments of Mark B. Morrow rose to the top of each photo. He would take one look and list the year, make and model of every car in the photo. Easily this allowed me to put specific dates to the photos I was looking at. When I began work on this book I found I had a lot of photos of Shirley that were not dated. But these photos ... they had cars in them. So I contacted Mark B. Morrow and asked for his assistance. Which he was happy to provide. He is a truly incredible person and an indispensable resource when it comes to research.

12/2/22, 8:28 PM

There wasn't a lot to go on, but the few pieces of chrome trim were very helpful. The curved rear quarter panel, placement of the door lock under the handle shape of the handle and flat top of the vent window narrowed it down to '49-50 GM. The chrome line down the lower door and over the quarter panel points to 1949 Buick. While GM used the same doors across the lines, only Buick had the broad chrome strip all the way down the door and over the bulge of the quarter.

The white car in the backgrouns also looks to be a '49 Buick from what I can make out of the taillight. The door on the black car appears to be dented in. Maybe she was at the dealer for a repair estimate.

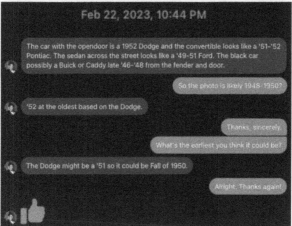

Feb 22, 2023, 10:44 PM

The car with the opendoor is a 1952 Dodge and the convertible looks like a '51-'52 Pontiac. The sedan across the street looks like a '49-51 Ford. The black car possibly a Buick or Caddy late '46-'48 from the fender and door.

So the photo is likely 1948-1950?

'52 at the oldest based on the Dodge.

Thanks, sincerely.

What's the earliest you think it could be?

The Dodge might be a '51 so it could be Fall of 1950.

Alright. Thanks again!

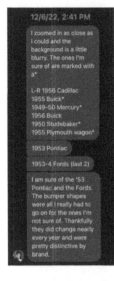

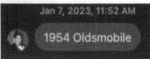

Genogram

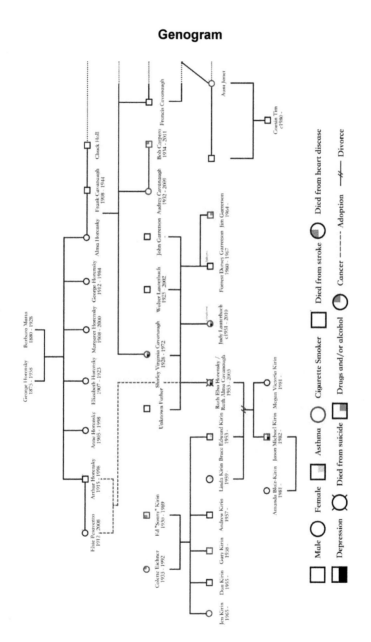

Photo Gallery

CURIOSITY SEEKERS JAM SHIRLEY'S HEARING   Crowds packed the
corridors leading to Judge Harry M. Montgomery's courtroom in a Roman
holiday atmosphere today as Shirley Cavanaugh, 28, accused of shooting
Police Lt. Allen Carnahan was led in by a deputy sheriff from the
County Jail.
              The Pittsburgh Press 3/7/57

OUT ON BOND IN COP-SHOOTING CASE is Shirley Cavanaugh, who is seen here at a hearing in No. 1 police station with two officers. She is charged with the felonious shooting with intent to kill in the wounding of Lt. Allen Carnahan in an after-hours club.

The Pittsburgh Press 2/27/57

SUSPECT AT POLICE STATION — Shirley Cavanaugh, 28, a woman of many
aliases and many addresses, walks through the cellblock door at
Penn Avenue police station after her surrender to the authorities
in the shooting of the City's narcotics squad boss.
2/27/57 Pittsburgh Press

PSP 2/26/57 PITTSBURGH: Shirley Cavanaugh, below, accused by Police
Lt. Allen Carnahan as the woman who shot him. Earlier Lt. Carnahan
said the shooting was an accident. KDKA-TV DO NOT USE UNITED PRESS
TELEPHOTO FROM FILES.

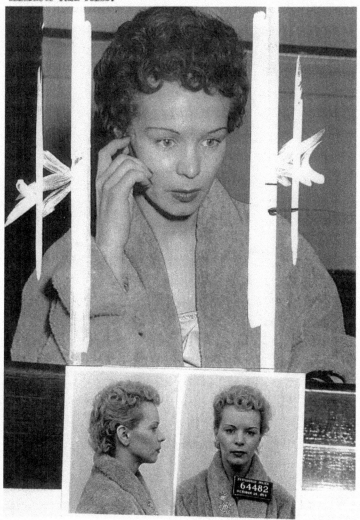

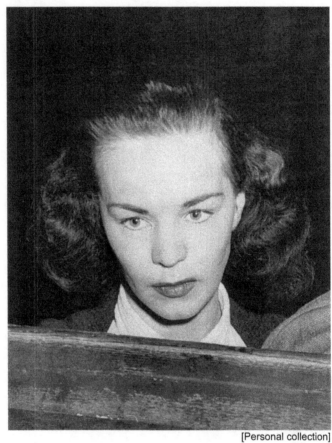

83

[Personal collection]

---

[83] I imagine this photo came from the 1996 family research but there was no label with it.

84

[Personal collection]

---

[84] This picture is one of the more haunting ones to me. If I catch this photo out of the corner of my eye, I see either my sister or my mother, but never Shirley.

707 Penn St. Braddock, PA. Shirley's childhood home

85

---

[85] Megan and I spent a day visiting old Shirley spots and taking pictures. I love that I got the chance to include this in this book.

Shirley's steps, Ardmore Blvd

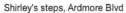

[Personal collection]

86

[Personal collection]

---

[86] Another favorite. Shirley with her friends. At, what appears to possibly be, a restaurant around Christmas time. I often wonder if these women were also sex workers. Furthermore I wonder … were they the "friends of Shirley" that helped take care of my mother when she was a baby?

[Personal collection]

---

[87] When I found this photo it was severely damaged. Multiple scratches. Black and white and tarnished. But it was Shirley's wedding day. I had to give her life. I had to take the scratches, take the blemishes, I had to care for her. I had to breathe color into her skin. I had to give her the beauty of life. Also, Stephen Lauterbach informed me this picture was taken in his grandmother's living room.

293

[Personal collection]

---

[88] This photo verifies that Shirley visited Kennywood Park at least twice. Which is wonderful.

[John Garretson personal collection]

---

[89] Thanksgiving with John Garretson and unidentified man. It makes my heart burst knowing how much love she got to experience after the Carnahan Affair.

SHIRLEY CAVANAUGH

... *changed her mind on "guilty" plea*

Sun-Telegraph Photo by John Alexandrowicz

Pittsburgh Sun-Telegraph, Thurs. Aug. 29, 1957

---

[90] Unfortunately Linda at the Post-Gazette archives was unable to uncover the original of this photo. When I look at this photo, it's one of very few, that I can see my face in Shirley's face. I can see my eyes, my jaw.

[Personal collection]

---

[91] This is the one.

Bienville Street and Chartres Street, New Orleans, Louisiana

1997   2023

Contact and Social Media Info

Email Contact: ShadysideHistory@Gmail.com
- My first book was an in depth research project based on the history of Shadyside Pennsylvania titled, "From Farmland to Card Shop: A History of Shadyside Through the Windows of 5522 Walnut St." From there my research of Pittsburgh histories truly exploded. Contact for general questions or research inquiries.

Facebook: https://www.facebook.com/FromTheFurnaceWithLove
- The entire collection of legal documents and nearly 400 newspaper clippings are viewable in this Facebook Group.

Hashtag: #FromTheFurnaceWithLove

Dear Mom,

I miss you.

Milton Keynes UK
Ingram Content Group UK Ltd.
UKHW010722050224
437294UK00019B/918